SpringerBriefs in Economics

SpringerBriefs present concise summaries of cutting-edge research and practical applications across a wide spectrum of fields. Featuring compact volumes of 50 to 125 pages, the series covers a range of content from professional to academic. Typical topics might include:

- A timely report of state-of-the art analytical techniques
- A bridge between new research results, as published in journal articles, and a contextual literature review
- A snapshot of a hot or emerging topic
- An in-depth case study or clinical example
- A presentation of core concepts that students must understand in order to make independent contributions

SpringerBriefs in Economics showcase emerging theory, empirical research, and practical application in microeconomics, macroeconomics, economic policy, public finance, econometrics, regional science, and related fields, from a global author community.

Briefs are characterized by fast, global electronic dissemination, standard publishing contracts, standardized manuscript preparation and formatting guidelines, and expedited production schedules.

More information about this series at http://www.springer.com/series/8876

Petr Mariel · David Hoyos · Jürgen Meyerhoff ·
Mikolaj Czajkowski · Thijs Dekker ·
Klaus Glenk · Jette Bredahl Jacobsen ·
Ulf Liebe · Søren Bøye Olsen · Julian Sagebiel ·
Mara Thiene

Environmental Valuation with Discrete Choice Experiments

Guidance on Design, Implementation and Data Analysis

See next page

The authors are members of the ENVECHO group
(ENVironmEntal CHOice—www.envecho.com)

ISSN 2191-5504 ISSN 2191-5512 (electronic)
SpringerBriefs in Economics
ISBN 978-3-030-62668-6 ISBN 978-3-030-62669-3 (eBook)
https://doi.org/10.1007/978-3-030-62669-3

© The Author(s) 2021. This book is an open access publication.
Open Access This book is licensed under the terms of the Creative Commons Attribution 4.0 International License (http://creativecommons.org/licenses/by/4.0/), which permits use, sharing, adaptation, distribution and reproduction in any medium or format, as long as you give appropriate credit to the original author(s) and the source, provide a link to the Creative Commons license and indicate if changes were made.
The images or other third party material in this book are included in the book's Creative Commons license, unless indicated otherwise in a credit line to the material. If material is not included in the book's Creative Commons license and your intended use is not permitted by statutory regulation or exceeds the permitted use, you will need to obtain permission directly from the copyright holder.
The use of general descriptive names, registered names, trademarks, service marks, etc. in this publication does not imply, even in the absence of a specific statement, that such names are exempt from the relevant protective laws and regulations and therefore free for general use.
The publisher, the authors and the editors are safe to assume that the advice and information in this book are believed to be true and accurate at the date of publication. Neither the publisher nor the authors or the editors give a warranty, expressed or implied, with respect to the material contained herein or for any errors or omissions that may have been made. The publisher remains neutral with regard to jurisdictional claims in published maps and institutional affiliations.

This Springer imprint is published by the registered company Springer Nature Switzerland AG
The registered company address is: Gewerbestrasse 11, 6330 Cham, Switzerland

Petr Mariel
Department of Quantitative Methods
University of the Basque Country,
UPV/EHU
Bilbao, Spain

Jürgen Meyerhoff
Institute of Landscape Architecture
and Environmental Planning
Technische Universität Berlin
Berlin, Germany

Thijs Dekker
Institute for Transport Studies
University of Leeds
Leeds, UK

Jette Bredahl Jacobsen
Department of Food and Resource
Economics
University of Copenhagen
Frederiksberg, Denmark

Søren Bøye Olsen
Department of Food and Resource
Economics
University of Copenhagen
Frederiksberg, Denmark

Mara Thiene
Department of Land, Environment,
Agriculture and Forestry
University of Padua
Padua, Italy

David Hoyos
Department of Quantitative Methods
University of the Basque Country,
UPV/EHU
Bilbao, Spain

Mikolaj Czajkowski
Department of Economics
University of Warsaw
Warsaw, Poland

Klaus Glenk
Central Faculty, SRUC
Department of Rural Economy,
Environment and Society
Edinburgh, UK

Ulf Liebe
Department of Sociology
University of Warwick
Coventry, UK

Julian Sagebiel
Department of Economics
Swedish University of Agricultural Sciences
Uppsala, Sweden

Preface

Discrete choice experiments (DCE) are nowadays used in many areas, including environmental valuation. One reason for their popularity is that they are said to provide more detailed information for decision making, as compared with other stated preference (SP) methods. The outcome of a DCE in environmental valuation is not only a measure for the overall welfare effects of environmental changes caused, for example, by dyke relocations along rivers to create floodplains, but also provides additional insights into preferences for specific characteristics of the management action: the amount of floodplain area gained, whether the floodplains are forested or not, or whether the changes will impact on recreational opportunities. However, designing, carrying out, and analysing DCE is, in our experience, a more complicated process than employing other valuation methods such as the Contingent Valuation Method (CVM). Ensuring the validity and the reliability of the requested welfare estimates, therefore, requires awareness of the many factors that can have an impact on both.

Several publications are available that advise on how to conduct SP surveys, some including the application of DCE. We only mention a few here. Well known in the literature are the NOAA guidelines (Arrow et al. 1993), that were developed after the Exxon Valdez accident in 1989 and the heated debate that followed about whether damage to the environment could be assessed by using the CVM, the standard SP method at that time. The NOAA guidelines were intended to set standards so that estimates could be used for natural resource damage assessments. More recently are the good practice guidelines provided by Riera et al. (2012) (see also Riera and Signorello 2016). These authors established good practice protocols for the economic valuation of non-market forest ecosystem goods and services, covering the main valuation methods Hedonic Pricing, Travel Cost, Contingent Valuation, Choice Modelling and additionally Benefit Transfer. The most recent contribution is the paper by Johnston et al. (2017). This proposes contemporary best-practice recommendations for SP studies that aim to provide information for decision making. The document reflects the state of the art based on a thorough analysis of the literature and introduces the reader to many of the challenges of using SP surveys. Two other valuable sources for people who have to design and analyse DCE that should be mentioned here are the edited books by Kanninen (2007) and Champ et al. (2017).

The present book, however, is different and should not be seen as a substitute or update of available guidance documents, but as a complement. One reason for this is that it focuses exclusively on DCE, although some of the issues raised may also be applicable to CVM studies. While the overall structure of this manuscript mirrors the steps taken when conducting a DCE study, it may also be used as a reference book. Each of the topics is discussed concisely and can be understood without reading other contributions. Acknowledging previous guidance documents, the authors of this book felt that this kind of guidance would fill an existing gap in the literature. In our experience with PhD-students, although this is a widespread problem, they often struggle with practical questions concerning, for example, the number of attributes they can use in their DCE or the number of draws they should use when estimating a random parameter logit model. In this sense, the book aims to support researchers and practitioners who plan to conduct a DCE from the early design stages to later steps such as analysing the data and calculating welfare measures.

However, this book does not intend to assume responsibility for the decisions, required when designing and conducting a DCE study, which are taken by the reader. In contrast, it aims to raise awareness of the consequences of certain decisions made during the design process (e.g. the number of alternatives) or during the data analysis (e.g. dummy coding of some attributes). Moreover, the book does not seek to set standards on the right way to do certain things but to provide the reader with the knowledge and experience that we have gained through our research on DCE, especially as we are a group of academics who have met regularly over the last decade as members of the ENVECHO network (a scientific network of researchers using discrete choice modelling in the field of environmental valuation —www.envecho.com).

Overall, we hope that the experience we want to share with the readers helps them to carry out a DCE study and contributes to increasing the validity of SP studies available for environmental decision making. Finally, we wish that this book could initiate further research on the validity and reliability of DCE outcomes, including questioning the experience presented here.

Bilbao, Spain	Petr Mariel
Bilbao, Spain	David Hoyos
Berlin, Germany	Jürgen Meyerhoff
Warsaw, Poland	Mikolaj Czajkowski
Leeds, UK	Thijs Dekker
Edinburgh, UK	Klaus Glenk
Frederiksberg, Denmark	Jette Bredahl Jacobsen
Coventry, UK	Ulf Liebe
Frederiksberg, Denmark	Søren Bøye Olsen
Uppsala, Sweden	Julian Sagebiel
Padua, Italy	Mara Thiene

Acknowledgements The authors acknowledge support by the Open Access Publication Fund of Technische Universität Berlin, FEDER/Ministry of Science, Innovation and Universities through grant ECO2017-82111-R, the Basque Government through grant IT1359-19 (UPV/EHU Econometrics Research Group) and the National Science Centre of Poland (Sonata Bis, 2018/30/E/HS4/00388).

References

Arrow K, Solow R, Portney P, et al (1993) Report of NOAA Panel on contingent valuation. Federal Register 58:4601–4614

Champ PA, Boyle KJ, Brown TC (eds) (2017) A Primer on Nonmarket Valuation. Springer Netherlands, Dordrecht

Johnston RJ, Boyle KJ, Adamowicz W (Vic), et al (2017) Contemporary Guidance for Stated Preference Studies. Journal of the Association of Environmental and Resource Economists 4:319–405. https://doi.org/10.1086/691697

Kanninen BJ (ed) (2007) Valuing Environmental Amenities Using Stated Choice Studies: A Common Sense Approach to Theory and Practice. Springer Netherlands, Dordrecht

Riera P, Signorello G (2016) Valuation of forest ecosystem services. A practical guide, EUROFOREX – COST E45 report

Riera P, Signorello G, Thiene M, et al (2012) Non-market valuation of forest goods and services: Good practice guidelines. Journal of Forest Economics 18:259–270. https://doi.org/10.1016/j.jfe.2012.07.001

Contents

1 **Theoretical Background** 1
  1.1 Welfare Economics 1
  1.2 Random Utility Maximisation Model 4
  References 5

2 **Developing the Questionnaire** 7
  2.1 Structure of the Questionnaire 7
  2.2 Description of the Environmental Good 11
  2.3 Survey Pretesting: Focus Groups and Pilot Testing 14
  2.4 Incentive Compatibility 16
  2.5 Consequentiality 18
  2.6 Cheap Talk, Opt-Out Reminder and Oath Script 19
  2.7 Instructional Choice Sets 23
  2.8 Identifying Protesters 25
  2.9 Identifying Strategic Bidders 26
  2.10 Payment Vehicle and Cost Vector Design 27
  References 29

3 **Experimental Design** 37
  3.1 The Dimensionality of a Choice Experiment 37
    3.1.1 Number of Choice Tasks 38
    3.1.2 Number of Attributes 38
    3.1.3 Number of Alternatives 39
    3.1.4 Other Dimensionality Issues 39
  3.2 Statistical Design of the Choice Tasks 40
  3.3 Checking Your Statistical Design 44
  References 47

4 **Collecting the Data** 51
  4.1 Sampling Issues 51
  4.2 Survey Mode (Internet, Face-To-Face, Postal) 54
  References 58

5	**Econometric Modelling: Basics**		61
	5.1	Coding of Attribute Levels: Effects, Dummy or Continuous	61
	5.2	Functional Form of the Attributes in the Utility Function	63
	5.3	Econometric Models	66
		5.3.1 Multinomial (Conditional) Logit	66
		5.3.2 Mixed Logit Models—Random Parameter, Error Component and Latent Class Models	67
		5.3.3 G-MXL Model	69
		5.3.4 Hybrid Choice Models	69
	5.4	Coefficient Distribution in RP-MXL	70
	5.5	Specifics for the Cost Attribute	72
	5.6	Correlation Between Random Coefficients	73
	5.7	Assuring Convergence	74
	5.8	Random Draws in RP-MXL	76
	References		77
6	**Econometric Modelling: Extensions**		83
	6.1	WTP-Space Versus Preference Space	83
	6.2	Scale Heterogeneity	85
	6.3	Information Processing Strategies	87
	6.4	Random Regret Minimisation—An Alternative to Utility Maximisation	89
	6.5	Attribute Non-attendance	91
	6.6	Anchoring and Learning Effects	93
	References		95
7	**Calculating Marginal and Non-marginal Welfare Measures**		103
	7.1	Calculating Marginal Welfare Measures	103
	7.2	Aggregating Welfare Effects	106
	7.3	WTP Comparison	108
	References		109
8	**Validity and Reliability**		111
	8.1	The Three Cs: Content, Construct and Criterion Validity	111
	8.2	Testing Reliability	114
	8.3	Comparing Models	118
		8.3.1 Model Fit-Based Strategies to Choose Among Different Models	119
		8.3.2 Cross Validation	120
	8.4	Prediction	120
	References		121
9	**Software**		125
	References		128

Abbreviations

AIC	Akaike Information Criterion
BIC	Bayesian (Schwarz) Information Criterion
CVM	Contingent valuation method
DCE	Discrete choice experiment
DM-MXL	Discrete mixture model
G-MXL	Generalized mixed logit
ICS	Instruction choice set
LCM	Latent class model
LCRP-MXL	Latent class random parameters mixed logit
MNL	Multinomial logit
mWTP	Marginal willingness to pay
MXL	Mixed logit model
RP	Revealed preference
RP-MXL	Random parameters mixed logit
RRM	Random regret minimisation
RUM	Random utility maximisation
SP	Stated preference
WTA	Willingness to accept
WTP	Willingness to pay

Chapter 1
Theoretical Background

Abstract This chapter starts by briefly presenting the theoretical background of welfare economics and introducing key aspects such as the indirect utility function, the expenditure function, or the concepts of compensating surplus or equivalent surplus. Next, it draws attention to willingness to pay and willingness to accept, essential measures in environmental valuation. Finally, the chapter summarises the basic mathematical notation of the random utility maximisation models used throughout the book.

1.1 Welfare Economics

Environmental valuation departs from the assumption that the goods and services provided by nature can be treated as arguments of the utility function of each individual. The main purpose of environmental valuation is to obtain a monetary measure of the change in the level of utility of each individual as a consequence of a change in the provision of these goods and services (Hanemann 1984). These individual measures can subsequently be aggregated across society and compared against the costs of implementing the change and thereby inform policymakers whether the proposed change is value for money, or more formally constitutes a potential Pareto improvement to society (Nyborg 2014).

For this purpose, it is imperative to establish a link between utility and income. In microeconomic theory, this is achieved by assuming that an individual derives utility from consuming goods and services provided by nature (e.g. clean water or recreation). Individuals maximise utility subject to a budget constraint. Hence, income and prices together define the feasible set of consumption patterns. The outcome of this optimisation process is a set of (Marshallian) demand functions, where demand depends on income, prices and environmental quality. An important distinction that needs to be made is between direct and indirect utility. Direct utility is the utility obtained from consuming goods and is unconnected to prices and income. For a connection with income and prices, we thus need to look at changes in optimal behaviour. This is where indirect utility comes into play. That is, we know through the demand functions how individuals respond to price, income and quality changes. Hence, the term indirect utility represents the utility derived at the optimal demand levels. In the DCE literature, most authors refer to indirect utility functions when they mention utility functions.

Benefit estimation departs from inferring the net change in income that is equivalent to or compensates for changes in the quantity or quality in the provision of environmental goods and services (Haab and McConnell 2002). More formally, we start by defining an individual's direct utility function in terms of z, a vector of market commodities and q, a vector of environmental services:

$$u(z, q).$$

The individual may choose the quantity of z but q is exogenously determined. Further, the individual maximises utility subject to income, y, so that the problem can be reframed in terms of the indirect utility function, v:

$$v(p, q, y) = \max_{z}\{u(z, q) | p \cdot z \leq y\},$$

where p denotes the price of market goods. Similarly, the expenditure function associated with the utility change, which is the dual of the indirect utility function, can be defined:

$$e(p, q, u) = \min_{z}\{p \cdot z | u(z, q) \geq u\}.$$

The expenditure function defines the minimum amount of money an individual needs to spend to achieve a desired level of utility, given a utility function and the prices of the available market goods. The indirect utility function and the expenditure function provide the basic theoretical framework for quantifying welfare effects, having some useful properties: (1) the first derivate of the expenditure function with respect to price equals the Hicksian or utility constant demand function (also known as Shephard's lemma); (2) the negative of the ratio of derivatives of the indirect utility function with respect to price and income equals the Marshallian or ordinary demand curve (also known as Roy's identity); and (3) if the utility function is increasing and quasi-concave in q, the indirect utility function is also increasing and quasi-concave in q and the expenditure function is decreasing and convex in q. Finally, it is important to highlight that the above discussion relies on assuming that the indirect utility function is linear in prices and independent of income in order to arrive at a demand restricted to unity—i.e. what is commonly assumed in discrete choice models. For more in-depth discussion, interested readers may refer to Karlstrom and Morey (2003), Batley and Ibáñez Rivas (2013), Dekker (2014), Dekker and Chorus (2018) and Batley and Dekker (2019).

Welfare theory distinguishes two ways in which changes in environmental quality may affect an individual's utility: either by changes in the prices paid for marketed goods or by changes in the quantities or qualities of non-marketed goods. Although

1.1 Welfare Economics

essentially similar, the measures of welfare impact differ, being compensating variation and equivalent variation in the former and compensating surplus (CS) and equivalent surplus (ES) in the latter.

Given that most environmental policy proposals involve changes in either the quantities or the qualities of non-market environmental goods and services where q is exogenously determined for the individual, we will describe welfare measures in terms of CS and ES here. For cases where individuals can freely adjust their consumption of both z and q, interested readers may refer to Freeman et al. (2014) for similar deliberations of the compensating and equivalent variation measures.

If q changes, the individual's utility may increase, decrease or remain constant. The value of a welfare gain associated with a change in the environmental good from the initial state q^0 (usually known as *status quo*) to an improved state q^1 is defined in monetary terms by the CS

$$v(p, q^1, y - CS) = v(p, q^0, y) = v^0, \tag{1.1}$$

and the ES

$$v(p, q^1, y) = v(p, q^0, y + ES) = v^1 \tag{1.2}$$

It is important to note that even though CS and ES are both welfare measures of the same improvement in q, the two measures differ in their implied "rights" when income effects are present. The CS implies that the individual has the right to the status quo (i.e. the individual does not have the right to the improvement in q). Hence, the welfare gain is measured keeping utility fixed at v^0. On the other hand, the ES implies that the individual has the right to the change, and, hence, measures the welfare gain keeping utility fixed at v^1. This difference in definition leads to differences in how the CS and ES are measured in practice. CS for an improvement in q is measured by the monetary amount corresponding to the individual's maximum willingness to pay (WTP) to obtain the improvement. ES for an improvement in q is measured by the monetary amount corresponding to the individual's minimum willingness to accept (WTA) compensation for not obtaining the improvement. In other words, WTP and WTA are equivalent ways of measuring a welfare change: the change in income that makes a person indifferent to an exogenously determined change in the provision of an environmental good or service. The relationship between the Hicksian welfare measures and WTP/WTA is summarised in Table 1.1 for the welfare gain context described above, as well as for a welfare loss context, e.g. in terms of a deterioration of q.

The Hicksian welfare measures may be rewritten in terms of the expenditure function:

$$WTP = e(p, q^0, u^0) - e(p, q^1, u^0) \text{ when } u^0 = v(p, q^0, y),$$
$$WTA = e(p, q^0, u^1) - e(p, q^1, u^1) \text{ when } u^1 = v(p, q^1, y).$$

Table 1.1 The relationship between Hicksian measures and WTP/WTA

	Compensating surplus	Equivalent surplus
Definition	Amount of income paid or received that leaves the individual at the initial level of well-being	Amount of income paid or received that leaves the individual at the final level of well-being
Welfare gain	WTP	WTA
Welfare loss	WTA	WTP

Source Adapted from Haab and McConnell (2002)

It is important to denote that while WTP is bound by the income level, WTA is not. Even though WTP and WTA are welfare measures of the same change, theoretically as well as empirically they may differ substantially. This disparity has been found both in real markets and hypothetical markets and both for private and public goods. It has been argued that it can be influenced by many factors, such as income effects, transaction costs and broad-based preferences (Horowitz and McConnell 2002).

In theory, which welfare measure to use depends entirely on what is the most appropriate assumption to make concerning the property rights in the specific empirical case (Carson and Hanemann 2005). However, the current state of practice of environmental valuation tends to favour WTP measures as they are more conservative (i.e. specially the case in valuation studies for litigation processes) and for incentive compatibility issues arising when using WTA measures (as will be discussed in Sect. 2.4). However, WTA has been found to be a better approach in practice when applying non-market valuation techniques in low-income countries. So the decision to focus on WTP or WTA remains an area for further research, ultimately dependent on the purpose of the study.

Discrete choice models work with indirect utility functions, although practitioners should realise that these functions derive from direct utility functions. Restrictions are therefore in place, particularly in the context of the inclusion of price and income variables, to work back to the original utility maximisation problem. Despite being underexplored, the use of indirect utility functions that are linear in costs and income may be recommended for now.

1.2 Random Utility Maximisation Model

The theoretical model commonly used for analysing discrete choices is the random utility maximisation (RUM) model, based on the assumption of the utility-maximising behaviour of individuals. Under the RUM, an individual n out of N individuals faces a choice among J alternatives in one or T repeated choice occasions. The individual n obtains from an alternative j in a choice occasion t a certain level of indirect utility U_{njt}. For simplification purposes, the rest of the text will refer to this indirect utility function as simply utility function, as commonly done in the RUM literature.

1.2 Random Utility Maximisation Model

The alternative i is chosen by individual n in choice occasion t if and only if $U_{nit} > U_{njt}, \forall j \neq i$. The researcher does not observe the individual's utility but observes only some attributes related to each alternative and some characteristics of the individual. The utility U_{njt} is then decomposed as

$$U_{njt} = V_{njt} + \varepsilon_{njt}, \tag{1.3}$$

where ε_{njt} represents the random factors that affect U_{njt} but are not included in V_{njt}, often known as the deterministic (or representative) utility. The error ε_{njt} is assumed to be a random term with a joint density of the random vector denoted $f(\varepsilon_n) = f(\varepsilon_{n11}, \varepsilon_{n2}, \ldots \varepsilon_{nJT})$. The deterministic utility V_{njt} is usually assumed to be linear in parameters, that is $V_{njt} = x'_{njt}\beta$, where x_{njt} is a vector of variables describing goods or attributes of goods (including their price) that relate to alternative j and β which are unknown coefficients.

If the utility of all alternatives is multiplied by a constant, the alternative with the highest utility does not change. Therefore, the model

$$U_{njt} = V_{njt} + \varepsilon_{njt} = x'_{njt}\beta + \varepsilon_{njt} \tag{1.4}$$

is equivalent to

$$U^*_{njt} = \lambda V_{njt} + \lambda \varepsilon_{njt} = x'_{njt}(\lambda \beta) + \lambda \varepsilon_{njt}. \tag{1.5}$$

The normalisation of the model is usually achieved through the normalisation of the variance of the error terms. For example, in a logit model, the errors are *i.i.d.* type I extreme value distributed with location parameter zero and scale one (also called the Gumbel distribution). As the variance of this distribution is $\pi^2/6$, we are implicitly normalising the scale of utility. In the case of independently and identically distributed normal errors with variance one, leading to the independent Probit model, the scale of utility is, therefore, implicitly normalised to a different value (Train 2009, Chap. 3).

References

Batley R, Dekker T (2019) The intuition behind income effects of price changes in discrete choice models, and a simple method for measuring the compensating variation. Environ Resource Econ. https://doi.org/10.1007/s10640-019-00321-2

Batley R, Ibáñez Rivas JN (2013) Applied welfare economics with discrete choice models: implications of theory for empirical specification. In: Hess S, Daly A (eds) Choice modelling. Edward Elgar Publishing, pp 144–171

Carson RT, Hanemann WM (2005) Contingent Valuation. In: Mäler KG, Vincent JR (eds) Handbook of environmental economics, vol 2. Elsevier, pp 821–936. https://doi.org/10.03248/S1574-0099(05)02017-6

Dekker T (2014) Indifference based value of time measures for Random Regret Minimisation models. Journal of Choice Modelling 12:10–20. https://doi.org/10.1016/j.jocm.2014.09.001

Dekker T, Chorus CG (2018) Consumer surplus for random regret minimisation models. J Environ Econ Policy 7:269–286. https://doi.org/10.1080/21606544.2018.1424039

Freeman AMI, Herriges JA, Kling CL (2014) The measurement of environmental and resource values : theory and methods. Routledge

Haab TC, McConnell KE (2002) Valuing environmental and natural resources. The econometrics of non-market valuation. Edward Elgar Publishing Limited, Cheltenham, UK

Hanemann WM (1984) Discrete/continuous models of consumer demand. Econometrica 52:541–561. https://doi.org/10.2307/1913464

Horowitz JK, McConnell KE (2002) A review of WTA/WTP studies. J Environ Econ Manage 44:426–447. https://doi.org/10.1006/jeem.2001.1215

Karlstrom A, Morey ER (2003) Calculating the exact compensating variation in Logit and Nested-Logit Models with income effects: theory, intuition, implementation, and application. Social Science Research Network, Rochester, NY

Nyborg K (2014) Project evaluation with democratic decision-making: What does cost–benefit analysis really measure? Ecol Econ 106:124–131. https://doi.org/10.1016/j.ecolecon.2014.07.009

Train K (2009) Discrete choice methods with simulation, 2nd edn. Cambridge University Press, New York

Open Access This chapter is licensed under the terms of the Creative Commons Attribution 4.0 International License (http://creativecommons.org/licenses/by/4.0/), which permits use, sharing, adaptation, distribution and reproduction in any medium or format, as long as you give appropriate credit to the original author(s) and the source, provide a link to the Creative Commons license and indicate if changes were made.

The images or other third party material in this chapter are included in the chapter's Creative Commons license, unless indicated otherwise in a credit line to the material. If material is not included in the chapter's Creative Commons license and your intended use is not permitted by statutory regulation or exceeds the permitted use, you will need to obtain permission directly from the copyright holder.

Chapter 2
Developing the Questionnaire

Abstract This chapter outlines the essential topics for developing and testing a questionnaire for a discrete choice experiment survey. It addresses issues such as the description of the environmental good, pretesting of the survey, incentive compatibility, consequentiality or mitigation of hypothetical bias. For the latter, cheap talk scripts, opt-out reminders or an oath script are discussed. Moreover, the use of instructional choice sets, the identification of protest responses and strategic bidders are considered. Finally, issues related to the payment vehicle and the cost vector design are the subject of this section.

2.1 Structure of the Questionnaire

According to Dillman et al. (2008), a good questionnaire is like a conversation that has a clear, logical order. This includes to begin with easily understandable, salient questions and grouping-related questions with similar topics. Especially in web surveys, the initial questions have to be chosen carefully. Respondents cannot have a look at all the survey questions as with mail surveys and, therefore, the initial questions are crucial to get them interested in the survey. These questions should therefore apply to all respondents. Also, in the introduction to the survey respondents should be informed about the topic of the survey and give their consent to participate. There is evidence that an interesting survey topic can increase the response rate (Groves et al. 2004; Zillmann et al. 2014) and this can be taken into account in the introduction to the survey. While it is difficult to estimate a topic-related selection bias in survey participation, researchers should consider such a potential bias (e.g. Nielsen et al. 2016). For instance, it is more likely that a survey on environmental issues might be answered by individuals who are interested in environmental issues or have a high level of environmental concern. Such a potential bias could be reduced by making the survey and survey topic more general (e.g. quality of life in a region which also includes environmental issues).

In some surveys, respondents have to be screened out at the beginning of the survey because they do not belong to the target group. In this case, both eligible and ineligible respondents should be directed to the main survey after answering the screening questions in order to record non-response. Those who are ineligible should receive a thank you statement after being screened out.

It is a well-established fact that responses to survey questions can be affected by question context (Schuman et al. 1981; Tourangeau et al. 2000; Moore 2002; Dillman et al. 2008). Two types of context effects can be distinguished (Tourangeau et al. 2000, p. 198). First, a directional context effect is present if answers to a target question such as choice experiment tasks depend on whether context questions such as relevant attitudinal questions are placed before or after the target question. Second, a correlational context effect occurs if the correlation between responses to the target and the context questions is affected by the question order. The latter means, for example, that the relationship between attitude measurements and responses to choice tasks is affected by question order. Question context is likely to affect stated preferences because surveying relevant attitudes prior to choice tasks might provide an "interpretive framework" (Tourangeau and Rasinski 1988) with regard to the choice questions, leading to possible judgement effects (Tourangeau and Rasinski 1988, p. 306). There are only a few studies which have tested this type of context effects in SP surveys. Pouta (2004) showed in a contingent valuation study that the inclusion of relevant belief and attitudinal questions prior to the valuation question increases the likelihood that an environmentally friendly alternative is chosen and increases the respondents' WTP for environment forest regeneration practices in Finland. Liebe et al. (2016) find positive evidence for a directional context effect in a choice experiment study on ethical consumption. Therefore, when constructing a questionnaire it is important to be aware of this and consider possible implications of the fact that stated preferences and corresponding WTP estimates are likely to be affected by whether relevant attitudes are surveyed before or after the choice tasks in the experiment. In some cases, it may be considered relevant to ensure that respondents have thought about their own attitudes before answering the preference eliciting choice tasks, in other cases not.

Since respondents should be able to make informed decisions in line with their interests, the hypothetical market has to be described in as much detail as possible. This does not mean overloading respondents with information but naming the most important characteristics of the market context. Table 2.1 gives an overview of these characteristics (see Carson 2000, p. 1415 for contingent valuation) as well as a structure of a typical choice experiment questionnaire for environmental valuation.

When asking for preferences of unfamiliar goods or services, researchers might want to place questions on attitudes, social norms, etc., prior to the choice tasks in order to make respondents think carefully about the topic before answering the choice questions (see Bateman et al. 2002, p. 150, who recommend asking attitudinal and opinion questions before the valuation section in contingent valuation surveys). On the other hand, the literature on context effects discussed above (e.g. Liebe et al. 2016) often suggests asking such questions after the choice tasks instead because answering questions which are relevant for the choice task might activate socially

2.1 Structure of the Questionnaire

desirable response behaviour or direct attention to specific choice attributes, which is probably unintended by the researcher. Therefore, researchers should consider the possibility of unintended context effects which can also apply to so-called warm-up questions or instructional choice sets before the actual choice tasks.

Socio-demographic questions including gender, age, education and income are generally asked at the end of the survey. This is typically recommended because they refer to personal and partly sensitive information. The income question is especially sensitive and often causes high item non-response and missing values. On the other hand, it is an important variable for economic valuation studies. One way to reduce item non-response is to first ask respondents for an exact income amount and in the event they refuse to answer or choose a do not know option, provide a list of income

Table 2.1 Structure of a typical DCE survey

Questionnaire section	Content/related questions
Information given in the introduction to the survey	• What is the aim of the survey? • Who is eligible to take part? • Who is conducting the survey? • To what extent is anonymity or confidentiality of survey responses guaranteed? • How are the results going to be used/disseminated? • Initial question(s) which are easy to understand and applicable to all respondents • How long will it take to answer the survey? • Is ethical approval obtained for the study? • How will the data be stored?
Behavioural questions	• How often have you visited the environmental good in question (e.g. a forest or a beach)? • Which activities did you undertake?
Introduction in which the context of the choice task is described	• What is the societal or environmental problem? • How is the environmental good at hand linked to it?
Detailed description of the environmental good at hand, the institutional setting and payment vehicle	• What are the attributes of the good and how can they vary? • Who is responsible for the provision of the good (public or private institution, etc.)? • How do respondents pay for the good (taxes, fees, contributions to a fund, etc.)?
Choice experiment tasks	• How many alternatives shall a choice task include? • When shall a status quo and/or opt-out option be included? • How many choice tasks shall be presented to a respondent?

(continued)

Table 2.1 (continued)

Questionnaire section	Content/related questions
Follow-up questions to the choice tasks	• How did the respondents make their choices? • What were the most important choice attributes? • How difficult was it to answer the choice tasks? • To what extent is protesting affecting choice behaviour?
Questions on relevant attitudes, norms, etc., which help to "explain" heterogeneity of stated preferences	• To what extent are the respondents in favour or disfavour of the environmental good at hand (i.e. specific attitudes)? • How much are they concerned about environmental protection (i.e. general attitudes)? • To what extent does the social environment reward paying for an environmental good (i.e. social norm)? • To what extent does a respondent perceive a moral obligation to pay for the good at hand (i.e. personal norm)?
Questions on the socio-demographic background	• What is the respondent's gender, age, education, income, etc.?

categories (Duncan and Petersen 2001). Alternatively, income bands can be used to increase the response rate to the income variable. Only if the study is based on a quota design socio-demographic questions (often gender, age and education) are typically asked at the beginning of the survey to control sample quota and to screen out respondents in case of filled sampling quotas.

Another aspect of questionnaire design that can influence survey participation and dropouts is the length of a questionnaire (Galesic and Bosnjak 2009). Typically, this also depends on the survey mode—face-to-face interviews can be longer than mail and web surveys (see Sect. 4.2). Clearly, shorter surveys (e.g. around 20 min) are preferred over longer surveys. For example, regarding web surveys it can be shown that the longer the stated survey length in the introduction to the survey the lower the likelihood of participating and completing the survey (Galesic and Bosnjak 2009). Likewise, it is often expected that difficult questions cause higher dropout rates. Furthermore, in longer questionnaires the answers to questions positioned later in the questionnaire can be less valid compared to positioning the same questions at the beginning of the questionnaire. It is also important to state a reliable survey length in the introduction to the survey.

In summary, researchers need to be aware that all aspects of the questionnaire can affect the results of a DCE survey. A well-designed introduction to the survey can reduce non-response (unwillingness to participate) and selection (participation of specific individuals) bias. The question order can have an influence on choice experiment results. It is therefore important to consider unintended context effects,

2.1 Structure of the Questionnaire   11

for example, that environmental attitudes surveyed before the choice tasks might affect responses to the choice tasks, which might or might not be in the interest of the researchers. Also, warm-up questions or instructional choice sets can cause unintended anchoring effects, starting point effects, etc. While the ("optimal") length of a questionnaire also depends on the survey mode, it can be recommended to aim for shorter questionnaires (e.g. around 20 min), which not only increase survey participation, but also positively affect the validity and reliability of survey responses. The books by Dillman et al. (2008, 2014) are recommended as a comprehensive and detailed introduction to survey and questionnaire design.

2.2 Description of the Environmental Good

In addition to generic issues regarding how ordering may affect the answers to other questions (Sect. 2.1) another central issue is how much, and which information, to provide to respondents before presenting the choice sets. The basic principle is that a clear, unambiguous description (including time, scope, etc.) of the good to be valued is always required.

In many environmental valuation settings, valuation is conducted for a specific policy, resulting in a marginal change in the provision of certain goods. Describing the policy is therefore an important part of setting the context of the hypothetical market. The researcher typically wants respondents to perform trade-offs in a specific situation—e.g. evaluating policy proposals or choices of recreational actions. In order to make such choices, respondents need to be informed on what the choice is about. This involves explaining the *policy context* (the overall aim), the *environmental consequences* it will have (as also explained by the attributes) and how the *hypothetical market* is set up (e.g. how payment is to be made).

In principle, we want respondents to represent the target population, i.e. we should not provide any information at all if they also make uninformed decisions in real life—as it is well known that information affects choices (Jacobsen et al. 2008). On the other hand, we would like people to make informed choices: if the results should inform policymakers, they should reflect the preferences of people and most people would be likely to seek information before making choices. But the level of information sought may vary widely as we already know from real referenda.

A good starting point for deciding how and to what extent respondents should be informed is to think about the amount and quality of information people might already have prior to the survey. In the case of a local good, many people might already be familiar with it and also with its present quality and if so, little information may be enough. In case of a unfamiliar endangered species to be protected on a different continent obviously this might be different, suggesting that more information is needed. The risk of too much information is biasing people, the risk of too little is that if respondents do not have sufficient information on the good, they may use their imagination and hence different respondents end up valuing different "goods". Often we are in situations where we would like to provide a lot of information to respondents for them to make informed choices. But how much is enough? There is no clear answer to that. Pre-tests and focus groups can help to clarify this. The more unfamiliar a good and the less tangible it is, the more information is needed for them to make choices concerning a specific change. It may also differ depending on people's previous knowledge. A few examples may illustrate this: (1) working with farmers' willingness to change practices typically requires little information about the goods as they are well aware of their management practices and what they obtain from them, on the other hand, they may require more information on the instruments by which the practices have to be changed (e.g. Vedel et al. 2015a, b). Especially if we are working in developing countries with weak institutional settings (Nielsen et al. 2014; Rakotonarivo et al. 2017) it may require some effort to describe the hypothetical market (see, e.g., Kassahun and Jacobsen 2015). Working with recreational preferences in Western Europe often requires little information about the good and the hypothetical market, typically information on distance, as do preferences for environmental characteristics of food choices. Working with unfamiliar nature like deep water coral reefs requires a lot of information as many people have never heard about them (Aanesen et al. 2015).

A challenge with providing information is to ensure that people read it and digest it. Especially with online surveys, this is a big problem. Therefore, we often see that information is interrupted with attitudinal questions or questions about people's knowledge even though this may lead to context effects as mentioned in Sect. 2.1. For example, the description of the extent of a specific nature area may be accompanied with a question about whether people have visited the area or know the characteristics described. This may make them think specifically about this area and not nature areas in general (an intentional directional context, also referred to as framing), but can potentially bias them in terms of making them think more about recreational values than existence values. These kinds of trade-offs are important to consider and to test in focus groups and pre-survey interviews (see Sect. 2.3).

In the description explaining the environmental good, the hypothetical market and the policy situation, it is important to make the following points clear to respondents:

(a) That the proposed policy change leads to a certain outcome and that there is at least some scientific evidence for this relationship. A few examples may be: setting aside forests as a means of increasing the likelihood of securing the survival of endangered species; afforestation as a means of achieving greater carbon sequestration than the alternative land use under consideration, implementing restrictions on fertilisers in agriculture to affect water quality in nearby streams, etc. Notice that the relationship needs to be described as objectively as possible—both for validity and also to ensure that respondents are not protesting because they do not believe the given stated consequences. A particular challenge here is that the precise and objective description of these often quite complex biological relationships also has to be conveyed in layman's terms to be understandable to all respondents. In most cases, this requires careful testing in consecutive focus group interviews.

2.2 Description of the Environmental Good

(b) That it is generally important to distinguish means from outcomes, and most often we do this after valuing the outcome (as the means can be assessed as a cost). But a challenge occurs if the proposed means to achieve a particular outcome has positive/negative side effects, e.g. creation/destruction of local jobs, or regulating invasive species by "inhuman" means. These are important to identify in focus groups and through interviews with experts, and if present, attempt to avoid them in the description, or use a specific attribute to eliminate the effect on other attributes—even if this attribute in itself is of little interest.

(c) That the proposed policy change leading to a particular outcome is perceived as realistic by respondents. Quite often describing the scientific basis (as mentioned in point a) can be challenging. It is also important that the relationship of what is being valued is related to aspects that matter to the respondent. A classic example is valuing water quality, where a possible measure is N-concentration. Nevertheless, to relate it to a value that matters to people it has to be translated into the final ecosystem services being provided which are those presumably affecting people's utility, e.g. clarity of water for swimming, effect on biodiversity, etc. (see, e.g., Jensen et al. 2019).

(d) That the ones described to carry out the policy also have the power to do so—i.e. that the institutional setting is realistic.

(e) That the scope of the change is made explicit. In the contingent valuation literature this has been strongly emphasised. In DCE, it has often drawn less attention as the attributes vary and thereby internal scope sensitivity is ensured. But to make sure that respondents understand this well, it is necessary to be quite specific about the scope of the project/project combination proposed.

(f) That the attribute and attribute levels are well defined and explained in an understandable setting.

(g) That attributes should vary independently from each other if possible. This can often be a problem in, for example, conservation, where endangered species conservation and habitat restoration are correlated. An example of distinguishing these is Jacobsen et al. (2008) who has an attribute related to the area conserved, and then an attribute of ensuring survival of endangered species. For this to be realistic to respondents (and according to the natural science basis), respondents were told that it would be possible because other management initiatives targeted endangered species. This may in fact be possible as illustrated in a conservation strategy paper using the same valuation data as input (Strange et al. 2007).

(h) That the payment vehicle is well described (see Sect. 2.10).

(i) That consequentiality is ensured (see Sect. 2.5) and as far as possible also incentive compatibility (see Sect. 2.4).

In conclusion, content validity (see Sect. 8.1) requires a precise description of the environmental consequences, the policy to be implemented and the hypothetical market in a sufficiently detailed way so that respondents can make informed choices. This has to be weighted carefully with the risk of biasing people if information is not objective, or if a certain aspect of the good is emphasised over others. Thorough focus group and pilot testing are essential tools to find this balance.

Finally, another important issue not really touched on here is how information is conveyed to respondents. Most often information is provided through text and sometimes accompanying pictograms or images. Recently, several studies have started to use other media, for example, virtual environments (Bateman et al. 2009; Matthews et al. 2017; Patterson et al. 2017; Rid et al. 2018) or videos (Sandorf et al. 2016; Lim et al. 2020; Rossetti and Hurtubia 2020). To investigate whether those formats are more suitable to inform respondents about the good in question and the organisation of the hypothetical market is an open question requiring further research.

2.3 Survey Pretesting: Focus Groups and Pilot Testing

The development of SP surveys, as with all primary data-collection methods, requires devoting a substantial part of the overall work to designing and testing. Often this will be an iterative process that should use, among others, face-to-face pilot testing. Much effort should be devoted to translating expert knowledge into understandable and valuable information for respondents. Previous scientific investigation on the environmental characteristics of the good or service under valuation, expert advice and focus groups may facilitate the definition of attributes and levels of provision (Hoyos 2010). In this context, survey pretesting emerges as a basic prerequisite for a proper survey design (Mitchell and Carson 1989; Arrow et al. 1993; Johnston et al. 2017), including both qualitative (personal interviews or focus groups) and quantitative (pilot studies) pretesting. The main purpose of pretesting the survey is ensuring that the information provided in the questionnaire is sufficient, understandable and credible to the population, acknowledging that they may have different education levels and backgrounds. It is especially important to check that the environmental change, policy situation and hypothetical market (i.e. those highlighted in the previous section) are clear to respondents. Pretesting the survey also helps ensure the content validity of the questionnaire, as will be discussed in Sect. 8.1.

Testing the survey questionnaire generally involves four different methods: focus groups, cognitive interviews, group administrations and pilot surveys. Focus groups are small group (6–12 individuals) semi-structured, open-ended discussions among the relevant population. They facilitate the discussion of the concepts and language presented in the questionnaire and they are specifically useful in clarifying scenario and alternatives description, as well as evaluating the adequacy of the amount and level of information that respondents require in order to answer the valuation questions. Focus groups may also help when deciding the best strategy for explaining the task of making successive choices from a series of choice sets. Cognitive interviewing refers to questioning single individuals about his or her understanding and reactions to the questionnaire. Typically, concurrent verbal protocols are elicited from individuals in order to assess their understanding and reaction to the questionnaire. These protocols are especially useful to analyse respondents' reactions to specific sets of

2.3 Survey Pretesting: Focus Groups and Pilot Testing

the text using their own words (Willis 2005). Group administrations are designed for larger groups of people to silently record their answers to the questionnaire read to them by a professional interviewer (Wright and Marsden 2010).

Finally, pilot surveys are small field data collection testing with a small sample of the population (usually 50–100 respondents). They are highly recommended in order to develop a DCE survey because (1) it is cost-efficient as it may help detect problems in the questionnaire before collecting the whole sample; (2) it may serve as preliminary statistical analysis of the data; and (3) it may also help with defining priors for an efficient experiment design, as will be discussed in Sect. 3.2 (Leeuw et al. 2008). It is important to plan how participants for these different formats are recruited. While it is often convenient to use, for example, students, the question is whether participants who are easy to recruit sufficiently reflect the target population of the main survey. Good pretesting requires that people from the target population are involved in the pretesting phases.

Feedback from the respondents should be iteratively used in the revision of the questionnaire. Number of attributes and levels, payment vehicle and duration should be chosen in consonance with the good under valuation and its context. The analyst should weigh up the relevant number of attributes and the complexity of the design. The trade-off between the possibility of omission of relevant attributes and task complexity and cognitive burden to respondents may be analysed in focus groups and pilot surveys. Additionally, it may be interesting to use pre-tests to identify any possible interaction effect between attributes. Complexity of the choice task can be investigated with verbal protocols (Schkade and Payne 1994). In order to avoid group effects (Chilton and Hutchinson 1999), one-on-one interviews are also highly recommended (Kaplowitz and Hoehn 2001). With eye-tracking and other biometric sensor technology becoming increasingly affordable, it may be beneficial to supplement cognitive one-on-one interviews with such measures in order to acquire even more feedback on how respondents react to the information and questions presented to them in a questionnaire.

There is no fixed number of pre-tests of the survey that should be carried out because it may depend on the purpose of the study, the unfamiliarity of the good to be valued and the relative success of previous iterations, but current best practice recommends a minimum of four to six focus groups (Johnston et al. 2017). In cases like the BP Deepwater Horizon oil spill, for example, up to 12 focus groups, 24 cognitive interviews, 8 group administrations and 5 pilot surveys were conducted between mid-2010 and the end of 2013 for pretesting the questionnaire (Bishop et al. 2017). This is however an extreme case probably reflecting the largest amount of pretesting conducted in any SP survey. While the amount of pretesting needed is inherently case-specific and depends on the purpose for acquiring value estimates, for most environmental DCEs around 2–8 focus groups, 5–10 cognitive one-on-one interviews, and 1–2 pilot surveys would be considered sufficient.

Practitioners should bear in mind that proper pretesting of the survey requires time and, especially, resources for recruiting or rewarding participants, so that a specific budget for this purpose should be made available. It is also important to denote that gathering a random group from the relevant population may require the pretesting of the survey in different locations when the market size is large (e.g. a nationwide survey). Some guides to methods of collecting data for testing the questionnaire include Morgan (1997), Krueger and Casey (2008) and Dillman et al. (2008). Finally, survey pretesting should be properly documented and made available for reviewing purposes.

2.4 Incentive Compatibility

Incentive compatibility is the process in which a truthful response to a question constitutes the optimal strategy for an agent (Carson and Groves 2007). This means that respondents should find it in their best interest to answer truthfully. And by construction this is problematic for hypothetical choices—because will it ever have an impact what respondents answer? If I am asked whether I would prefer to die in a car accident or from cancer, it is not incentive compatible: my answer will not affect my probability of dying from either. Nor is it a choice I will be in a situation to make. Therefore, I have no incentive to answer honestly. And when respondents do not have an incentive to answer honestly, we are not guaranteed to get honest answers reflecting the respondent's true preferences. Even worse, if they have an incentive to answer dishonestly (e.g. due to warm-glow giving), we may get very wrong answers. Incentive compatibility is found to be important in many empirical settings, and Zawojska and Czajkowski (2017) find in a review that when choices are incentive compatible, they are more likely to pass external validity tests.

To ensure incentive compatibility, Vossler et al. (2012) list the following requirements: (1) participants care about the outcome (see also Sect. 2.5), (2) payment is coercive—it can be enforced on everyone (see also Sect. 2.10), (3) a single binary (yes/no) question format is used, (4) the probability of project implementation is weakly monotonically increasing by the proportion of yes-voters. DCEs with more than a single choice set violate requirement number 3 and hence do not satisfy incentive compatibility conditions. Given that DCEs typically do not live up to the criteria of incentive compatibility, the question is how important it is? Therefore, various attempts can be made to investigate the importance of incentive compatibility.

One is to construct a provision rule: a mechanism can be constructed that ensures implementation of only one strategy and independence between choice sets. The latter is typically addressed in stated DCE by explicitly asking respondents to value the choice sets independently from each other.

Another possibility is to rely on only binary choice which can also be done in DCE (e.g. Jacobsen et al. 2008), but in such cases, only the first choice set is potentially incentive compatible, whereby little information is obtained from each individual. An approximation that is sometimes being used to ensure incentive compatible DCEs in experimental settings is to implement a premium mechanism that randomly draws one of the choice sets as the winner, and that policy is then implemented. In a setting of provision of a public good on a large scale this is problematic in practice and incentivised choices may be used instead. This is preferably related to the good in

2.4 Incentive Compatibility

question, but may also simply be a premium. Svenningsen (2019) is an example of the former. The incentive was formulated at several places throughout the survey. In the beginning as:

> The survey you are participating in now is a bit different than the usual survey. As mentioned in the invitation-email you are given the opportunity to earn up to 18,000 extra points, the equivalent of 200 DKK, by participating in this survey. During the survey you can choose to donate all 200 DKK or some amount below the 200 DKK/18,000 points to climate policy. More information on this will follow later in the survey.

Then before the choice sets (and split up on several screens):

> As mentioned in the invitation-email, you are given 200 DKK, the equivalent of 18,000 points extra for your participation in this survey. In the choices you are about to make you are free to spend some part of or all 200 DKK as a donation towards implementing the climate policy you choose. You are free to choose the amount you wish to keep, as well as the amount you wish to donate towards climate policy. The amount not spent in this survey will be transferred to your account with Userneeds before the 18th of March 2016. You will be asked to make 16 choices and in each of these choices you have to imagine that you have the full 200 DKK/18,000 points that you either can donate or keep. One of your choices will be drawn at random and paid out and you will be informed about which choice it was at the end of the survey. The choices from all participants will be added up and the total amount donated will be used to buy and delete CO_2 quotas in the European quota-system, as well as donated to the UN Adaptation Fund. By buying and deleting CO_2 quotas the emissions of CO_2 is reduced. The researchers behind the survey will be in charge of these transactions. The amount used to buy CO_2 quotas and donated to the UN Adaptation Fund is determined through your choice of climate policy, as well as the choices of the other participants. You can read more about CO_2 quotas and the UN Adaptation Fund by following this link: https://www.adaptation-fund.org

> If you choose to donate, you have the option to receive certificates for the amount spent on buying and deleting CO_2 quotas, and the donations to the UN Adaptation Fund, as documentation. For this purpose we will therefore ask for your email address later in the survey. It is your choice whether or not you wish to supply your email address or not. Remember that climate policy 1 and 2 always involve adaptation and also CO_2 reduction if it is indicated in the description of the policy. Please also remember that the financing of the climate policy will be through a donation from you. Please make each of the 16 choices as if you had 200 DKK available each time.

As we can see, it may be rather lengthy to formulate if the policy context is intangible. Furthermore, it violates the general recommendation of not using donations as a payment vehicle as it may include other utility components such as warm-glow giving (Andreoni 1990). In conclusion, incentive compatibility is found to be important in empirical settings, yet DCE typically fails to satisfy its theoretical conditions due to the lack of single binary choices. It is always important to stress to respondents that choice sets are to be evaluated independently from each other. Furthermore, different ways to incentivise choices exist, e.g. with lotteries. While this is a possibility (see Palm-Forster et al. 2019 and Vossler and Zawojska 2020 for further discussion on the issue), it is not standard practice today.

2.5 Consequentiality

Consequentiality is defined by Carson and Groves (2007) as a situation in which a respondent thinks his/her answer can potentially influence the policy being investigated, whereby the answer to the survey is a possibility of influencing the policy—provided the policy is of interest to the respondent (see also Herriges et al. 2010 or Carson et al. 2014 for further discussion of this issue). This relates closely to the two first criteria mentioned with respect to incentive compatibility (see Sect. 2.4)—that respondents care about the outcome and that the payment can be enforced, but also to some extent with regard to the issue of binary questions—namely that it can be problematic to see an obvious outcome of several choices. The consequentiality issue in the literature is largely related to ensure that the answers to hypothetical questions can have an impact in the real world.

Within contingent valuation types of referenda, consequentiality has been investigated by, for example, Vossler and Evans (2009), who find that inconsequential questions lead to bias. The paper by Vossler et al. (2012) on consequentiality in DCE fundamentally shows that consequentiality on DCE is theoretically problematic as respondents answer multiple choice sets. Varying provision rules across split samples they find that this does not seem to be as important empirically.

Hassan et al. (2019) and Zawojska et al. (2019) distinguish between payment consequentiality and policy consequentiality, arguing that these two needs to be considered separately. Here, payment consequentiality is related to whether respondents believe that they will actually have to pay the cost of the chosen policy alternative if the policy is implemented in real life (i.e. free-riding is not possible). Policy consequentiality concerns whether respondents believe that their answers potentially influence the implementation of a policy, including whether the institution being paid has the institutional power to carry out the policy. In this regard, there is also the question of whether people trust that a policy has the described consequences, for example in terms of environmental improvements (Kassahun et al. 2016). Zawojska et al. (2019) find that policy and payment consequentiality have opposite effects on WTP, and therefore argue for them to be clearly distinguished and separately addressed.

For purely methodological DCE investigations, ensuring consequentiality may be challenging as the purpose of a study may be to learn more about the values of a certain good, but policy impact may be very far away. In these cases, it can be approached by telling respondents that the results of the survey will be communicated to politicians who may take it into account in their decision making. The more explicitly this can be done, the better. For example, it may be specified who will use this information and how it will be communicated. The more local a good is, and the more tangible, the easier it will often be to ensure such a communication and consideration.

If a survey is carried out on behalf of certain interest organisations or ministries (many studies are), policy consequentiality is often easier. However, highlighting the parties interested in the study may also lead to strategic answers (e.g. overbidding if an NGO is behind the survey with no power to force payments). So in such

2.5 Consequentiality

cases specific awareness is to be given to payment consequentiality. Finally, respondents may distrust whether the stated environmental consequences will actually come about—i.e. outcome uncertainty. As we generally are after valuing an environmental improvement and not how this is obtained, it can lead to what we may call outcome or provision consequentiality (note, this is not a term used in the literature, and it is very similar in nature to the policy consequentiality described above). If such uncertainty is important—or important in people's minds, it will have to be addressed explicitly to avoid biasing the results by people's self-perceived probability estimates. Glenk and Colombo (2011) is an example in which an attribute is presented as uncertain and Lundhede et al. (2015) an example in which the policy is uncertain. One common approach to investigate perceptions of consequentiality is in follow-up questions, where we also test for strategic bidders and protest bidders (see Sects. 2.8 and 2.9). This means questions explicitly stating to what degree they think they would actually pay, to what degree they think politicians will be informed and take in the information (see, e.g., Oehlmann and Meyerhoff 2017).

In summary, consequentiality is mainly handled by the way the policy, the payment and the outcome are described. This has to be done in a clear way that is also perceived as realistic. Current practice is to highlight communication plans of the project in the survey to provide policy consequentiality. Payment consequentiality is described further in Sect. 2.10. Furthermore, follow-up questions on people's perception of consequentiality may be used. The importance of consequentiality and how to ensure it is still under development.

2.6 Cheap Talk, Opt-Out Reminder and Oath Script

One type of ex ante script that has received considerable attention in the literature is the so-called Cheap Talk script originally developed by Cummings and Taylor (1999) for use in a study based on a referendum Contingent Valuation Method (CVM). Cheap Talk explicitly describes the problem of hypothetical bias to respondents prior to the preference elicitation. In three independent contingent valuation surveys (Cummings and Taylor 1999) effectively eliminated hypothetical bias using a rather lengthy script of around 500 words which, firstly, described the hypothetical bias phenomena, secondly, outlined some possible explanations for it, and, finally, asked respondents to vote in the following hypothetical referendum as if it were real.

While these results initially suggested that using Cheap Talk would be an effective approach to avoid hypothetical bias, results from a wide range of subsequent studies testing Cheap Talk in various CVM settings are ambiguous (List 2001; Aadland and Caplan 2003, 2006; Lusk 2003; Murphy et al. 2005; Nayga et al. 2006; Champ et al. 2009; Morrison and Brown 2009; Barrage and Lee 2010; Mahieu 2010; Ladenburg et al. 2010; Ami et al. 2011; Carlsson et al. 2011). Similarly, empirical tests in DCE settings have found ambiguous effectiveness of Cheap Talk (List et al. 2006; Ozdemir et al. 2009; Carlsson et al. 2010; Silva et al. 2011; Tonsor and Shupp 2011; Bosworth and Taylor 2012; Moser et al. 2014; Howard et al. 2015). While there has been no shortage of studies investigating Cheap Talk, it is relevant to note that most of these studies have used shorter scripts than the one originally used by Cummings and Taylor (1999). Despite the ambiguous results, it has become fairly common to include a Cheap Talk script when preparing questionnaires for empirical SP surveys. Exactly how common is difficult to assess, since details such as the inclusion or not of Cheap Talk (and other scripts) in questionnaires are not always reported when empirical survey results are published in scientific journals.

Johnston et al. (2017) note that the incentive properties of Cheap Talk are unclear, and it should thus not be applied without considering implications for framing and consequentiality. They further note that Cheap Talk directs the respondent's attention disproportionally to the costs, another aspect which requires caution. It would thus seem that Johnston et al. (2017) are generally sceptical towards using Cheap Talk in SP studies. However, it is not obvious that Cheap Talk as such is at odds with incentive compatibility and consequentiality. Considering the three overall parts of the full Cheap Talk script used by Cummings and Taylor (1999), the first part simply describing that people tend to overstate their WTP in hypothetical settings compared to real settings should not have adverse effects for incentive compatibility and consequentiality. The last part of the script, imploring respondents to answer as if it was a real choice situation, should also not have any adverse effects in this regard—on the contrary it encourages respondents to provide more truthful answers. The second part of the script, though, elaborating on possible reasons for hypothetical bias, could potentially be problematic if lack of incentive compatibility and/or lack of consequentiality are highlighted as potential reasons for hypothetical bias. As for the concern that Cheap Talk directs respondents' attention disproportionally towards the cost, it may be argued that this is exactly the purpose as hypothetical bias is essentially a result of respondents not paying as much attention to the cost in the hypothetical setting as they do in a non-hypothetical setting.

While few of the studies mentioned above have found Cheap Talk to completely remove hypothetical bias, most of them have found it to reduce hypothetical to at least some extent, and a few have found no effect at all. Only very few studies have found Cheap Talk to be outright counterproductive in terms of increasing hypothetical bias. Given that only two out of the more than 20 studies mentioned above find that using Cheap Talk actually leads to more biased WTP estimates than when Cheap Talk is not used, it would seem that for practical SP applications aimed at assessing WTP for non-marketed environmental goods the risk of introducing additional bias is outweighed by the greater chance of reducing bias. The actual impact will of course be context dependent and also depend on the specifics of the Cheap Talk script used. In relation to this it would seem that leaving out the second part of Cummings and Taylor's original script explaining the possible reasons for hypothetical bias would be favourable in order to avoid reducing survey consequentiality and incentive compatibility.

For self-administered survey modes, and in particular the increasingly used web surveys, where respondents due to limited attention budgets are likely to drop out or skip sections if faced with long text instructions (Lusk 2003; Bulte et al. 2005), using relatively short Cheap Talk scripts would seem preferable. These will typically be around 100 words in length. For example, a DCE-targeted short and neutral

2.6 Cheap Talk, Opt-Out Reminder and Oath Script

Cheap Talk script which avoids explaining to respondents about possible reasons for hypothetical bias might read as follows:

> In surveys like this, we often find that some people tend to overestimate or underestimate how much they are actually willing to pay for implementation of alternative environmental policies. Thus, they may choose alternatives that they would not actually prefer in real life. It is important that your choices here are realistic. Hence, in each of the following choice tasks, please consider carefully that your household is actually able and willing to pay the costs associated with the alternative you choose.

Recognising first of all that Cheap Talk was originally developed for CVM, and secondly that CVM and DCE are inherently structurally different from each other, Ladenburg and Olsen (2014) proposed that Cheap Talk might not sufficiently address the specific structures of DCE that might be subject to hypothetical bias. One aspect where DCE differs structurally from CVM is that respondents commonly have to answer multiple choice tasks. Inspired by the fact that, for instance, anchoring effects in DCE have been shown to be transient over a sequence of choice tasks (Bateman et al. 2008; Ladenburg and Olsen 2008) and learning effects have also been shown to affect choice behaviour over a sequence of choice tasks (Carlsson et al. 2012). Ladenburg and Olsen (2014) speculate that the effect of Cheap Talk might be transient in DCE in the sense the effect would wear off after a few choice tasks since respondents would at some point forget about the reminder. Howard et al. (2015) confirm this suspicion. Ladenburg and Olsen (2014) thus suggest the use of a so-called Opt-Out Reminder.

The Opt-Out Reminder is a small script that explicitly reminds respondents to choose the opt-out alternative if they find the proposed experimentally designed alternatives in the choice set to be too expensive. An example of an Opt-Out Reminder for a DCE with a zero-priced opt-out alternative defined as a continuation of the current environmental policy is the following: "*If you find the environmental policy alternatives too expensive relative to the resulting improvements, you should choose the current policy*".

The Opt-Out Reminder is displayed just before each single choice set to account for the repeated choice nature of DCE. Ladenburg and Olsen (2014) found that adding the Opt-Out Reminder to a survey design which included Cheap Talk leads to significant reductions in WTP estimates. Varela et al. (2014) also tested the impact of presenting an Opt-Out Reminder together with Cheap Talk. Contrary to Ladenburg and Olsen (2014), the Opt-Out Reminder was not found to influence WTP. A possible explanation might be that Ladenburg and Olsen (2014) repeated the Opt-Out Reminder before each single choice set whereas Varela et al. (2014) only presented it once in the middle of the choice task sequence. This seems to support Ladenburg and Olsen (2014) who speculate that, given the repeated choice nature of DCE, it may be of particular importance to repeat the reminder since respondents might otherwise forget about the reminder as they progress through the choice tasks. A major limitation of both Ladenburg and Olsen (2014) and Varela et al. (2014) is that they test the Opt-Out Reminder in a purely hypothetical set-up. Thus, they cannot assess the degree of hypothetical bias mitigation since no fully incentivised treatment is conducted. In a recent study, Alemu and Olsen (2018) test the repeated Opt-Out

Reminder in an incentivised set-up where Cheap Talk is not included. They find that the Opt-Out Reminder effectively reduces hypothetical bias to a substantial degree, though not completely removing it for all attributes. More empirical tests of the reminder are obviously warranted before its general applicability can be thoroughly assessed.

While the incentive properties of the Opt-Out Reminder are not entirely clear, considering the fact that the simple and very short script essentially just reminds respondents to be rational at the extensive margin, it would not per se be at odds with incentive compatibility or consequentiality. Before applying the Opt-Out Reminder one should also consider whether it attracts disproportional attention to the cost attribute relative to other attributes. Again, seeing disproportional attention to non-cost attributes as a main driver of hypothetical bias, Ladenburg and Olsen (2014) developed the wording of the Opt-Out Reminder with the specific intention of drawing more attention to the cost attribute. It is not entirely obvious what disproportional attention refers to when mentioned in Johnston et al. (2017) in relation to Cheap Talk. A reasonable interpretation would seem to be that it is relative to attention in real or incentivised choice settings. Hence, the concern would be whether the Opt-Out Reminder makes respondents focus much more on the cost in the hypothetical choice experiment than they would in real life, essentially over-correcting for hypothetical bias. Assessing this of course requires real or incentivised choice settings with which to compare. So far, Alemu and Olsen (2018) is the only empirical study in this regard. They find that the Opt-Out Reminder does not over-correct for hypothetical bias, suggesting that it does not attract a disproportional amount of attention to the cost attribute.

Another more recently proposed ex ante approach that has shown some effect in terms of reducing hypothetical bias is the use of a so-called Oath Script or Honesty Priming exercises that encourage respondents to be truthful when stating their preferences. While the Oath Script directly asks respondents to swear an oath that they will truthfully answer the value eliciting questions, Honesty Priming is a somewhat more subtle approach that seeks to subconsciously prime respondents to answer truthfully but subjecting them to words that are associated with honesty. Carlsson et al. (2013), de-Magistris and Pascucci (2014), Jacquemet et al. (2013, 2017) and Stevens et al. (2013) find that the Oath Script effectively mitigates hypothetical bias. In a similar vein, de-Magistris et al. (2013) found Honesty Priming to mitigate hypothetical bias in a laboratory setting, but Howard et al. (2015) was not able to confirm this effect when testing this approach in a field setting.

The body of research investigating these approaches to induce honesty is far less extensive as is the case for Cheap Talk. Johnston et al. (2017) note that the behavioural impacts of these approaches are not yet well understood and may therefore have unintended consequences, and they basically end up recommending more research into this. This is underlined by the fact that these approaches are not (yet) commonly used in practice.

The NOAA panel (Arrow et al. 1993) strongly recommended reminding respondents both of relevant substitute commodities as well as budget constraints. They furthermore noted that this should be done forcefully and just before the valuation questions. In an empirical test, Loomis et al. (1994) found no impact of providing budget and substitute reminders. These findings, however, lead to a series of comments and replies in Land Economics in the years that followed (Whitehead and Blomquist 1999), indicating that there may be some effect from these reminders. Substantial literature has developed assessing the importance of substitute reminders, but mainly addressing it from a framing or embedding angle (Hailu et al. 2000; Rolfe et al. 2002; Jacobsen et al. 2011). It is not clear from the literature how much budget and substitute reminders have been used in practice, maybe because it has not been common practice to report the use of these reminders. Hailu et al. (2000) noted that few CVM studies had followed these NOAA recommendations up until the year 2000.

To sum up, there is no clear recommendation for DCE practitioners whether or not to use *ex ante* framing methods such as the above-mentioned Cheap Talk scripts, Opt-Out Reminders, Oath Scripts, Honesty Priming scripts, Budget Reminders or Substitute Reminders to reduce or eliminate hypothetical bias. For some of these, more investigations are needed in order to make solid conclusions, even though this is no guarantee for obtaining clear recommendations. Cheap Talk has been thoroughly scrutinised in the literature, but results are ambiguous, causing disagreement among DCE researchers concerning whether Cheap Talk should be used at all. At the end of the day, it is up to the DCE practitioner to decide on a case-by-case basis whether to use any of these *ex ante* framing methods. Ideally, if incentive compatibility and consequentiality has been ensured, hypothetical bias should not be a concern, and there would be no need for these approaches. However, in practice, in most cases it is not possible to secure these conditions in environmental DCE surveys, which means that hypothetical bias is likely to present a serious—and in most practical cases untestable—validity concern. In these cases, the practitioner should at least consider the pros and cons of the various *ex ante* framing methods, and for the particular empirical case and setting consider whether using one or more of them in combination is most likely to bring the elicited estimates of value closer to the true values or rather move them further away. Overall, the empirical evidence in the literature suggests that the latter rarely happens.

2.7 Instructional Choice Sets

Most people who respond to choice tasks in a DCE survey questionnaire are likely to face this kind of questionnaire for the first time. The unfamiliarity can mean that, at least among some respondents, the degree of randomness is larger in the first choice tasks than in subsequent ones (Carlsson et al. 2012). In a dichotomous choice CVM context, Carson et al. (1994) suggested providing respondents with "warm-up" choice tasks in order to reduce the experienced uncertainty related to unfamiliar question context. Thus, in a couple of DCE surveys, respondents are presented a so-called instructional choice set (ICS) before they enter the sequence of choice tasks that will be used for estimating models and calculating WTP estimates (Ladenburg and Olsen 2008). Sometimes the former are also called training choice tasks while the latter are called value-elicitation choice tasks. The idea behind showing an ICS is to promote institutional learning, i.e. that respondents become more familiar with the choice context, the offered good and the choice tasks (see also Abate et al. 2018; Scheufele and Bennett 2012). The expected effect is that the ICS will reduce the degree of randomness that already exists among the first choices and thus improve the quality of choices recorded in the survey.

However, the literature has not provided clear evidence yet that the expected benefits from using an ICS, i.e. reducing the randomness of choices, will actually be achieved. At the same time, there are indications that the design of the ICS, especially the attribute level values shown on the ICS, might influence subsequent choices (e.g. Meyerhoff and Glenk 2015). This can happen, for example, because the attribute level values shown on the ICS might raise expectations and can, through anchoring, have an impact on all subsequent choices. Therefore, the overall effect of including an ICS might even be negative.

Given that the present evidence regarding the potential effects of an ICS is not yet conclusive, the following might be considered. Respondents generally get used to the choice task format quickly (Carlsson et al. 2012), an indicator of this is the often rapidly decreasing response time for a choice task as respondents move through the sequence of choice tasks (Meyerhoff and Glenk 2015). Thus, an ICS might not be that important. Instead, it is important that the order of appearance of the choice tasks a respondent faces is randomised. This way, not all respondents will have the same choice task as their first task and the potential anchoring effects, while still present, will now be dispersed over the full range of attribute levels rather than attached to one specific set of attribute levels. Even if the design is blocked, i.e. those who are assigned to different blocks face a different first choice task, it is essential to randomise the order of appearance to even up potential ordering effects.

If, however, an ICS is considered indispensable for reducing, for example, institutional uncertainty as the choice tasks are very complex and difficult to capture, the attribute level values shown on the ICS should be selected carefully. As these values could affect subsequent choices it seems advisable to avoid extreme values, i.e. the attribute level values representing the worst or best quality in your design, and level values in the middle of your attribute level range should be used. Especially very low values for cost in combination with levels of non-monetary attributes representing high quality levels might raise expectations that "you don't have to spend a lot in order to get high quality". Therefore, respondents might wait for similar alternatives and, as a consequence, the share of status quo choices could increase. In the event the attribute displays one of the highest levels available from among the range of cost levels, it could mean that those who have seen high price levels on the ICS do not trust that good quality can also be achieved at low costs. One option is to randomly select the attribute levels on the ICS so that numerous respondents see differently composed ICS. Another way to mitigate potential effects of anchoring could be to

2.7 Instructional Choice Sets

randomly draw a choice task from your experimental design so that the ICS differs across all respondents (Uggeldahl 2018).

2.8 Identifying Protesters

Protest responses are those systematically choosing the status quo option in a DCE, thus rejecting or protesting against some aspect of the constructed market scenario (Meyerhoff and Liebe 2006). In order to detect them, follow-up questions on the reasons for their answers are usually added to the valuation questions. Given that protest responses may lead to inconsistent welfare estimation, the researcher should properly detect and treat them (Meyerhoff and Liebe 2010).

Common identification approaches to protest answers include the use of debriefing questions, statistical outlier analysis and identification of systematic patterns in a set of choice situations. A typical debriefing question to identify zero protesters is to present a list of predetermined statements to respondents who consistently choose the zero-priced opt-out alternative throughout the choice set sequence, and ask which of these statements best corresponds to the reason why they always chose the opt-out. The list should include a range of statements of which some should indicate valid zeros (i.e. the choices are made in line with random utility maximisation, reflecting true preferences) while others should indicate protest zero (i.e. the choices made do not reflect the respondent's true preferences for the described good). When developing the list of statements, it is important to carefully consider the interpretation and classification of each statement to avoid ambiguous statements that afterwards cannot be clearly classified as a protest or valid. Usually protest answers take the form of beliefs that others (governments, private companies, etc.) are responsible and that they should bear the costs. As an example, the following statements can be used; ultimately they may depend on the context (Table 2.2).

Some authors have suggested it is better to use open-ended questions for the motives behind protest answers and then code them, which could lower the protest rate

Table 2.2 Items used for identifying protesters

Indicating protest	Indicating valid zero WTP
I do not want to put a dollar value on protecting nature	Society has more important problems than protecting plants and animals
Someone else should pay to protect natural resources	I cannot afford to pay
Not enough information is given	I do not think protecting plants and animals is worth the specified price
I object to the way the question is asked	I already spend a lot on animal welfare initiatives
The payment method is inappropriate	

Adapted from Meyerhoff and Liebe (2006, 2010) and Frey and Pirscher (2019)

(see, e.g., Bateman et al. 2002). It is also important to distinguish protest responses (e.g. "I don't want to put a dollar value on protecting plants and animals" from genuine zeros (e.g. "I can't afford to pay" or "I don't want to pay"). It has also been argued that those who are willing to pay may still hold some protest beliefs (Jorgensen and Syme 2000; Meyerhoff and Liebe 2006).

Statistical treatment of these responses includes dropping observations, sensitivity analysis to determine their impact on welfare measures, or using specific choice models able to accommodate protest responses (e.g. Meyerhoff et al. 2012). Sample selection models have also been proposed in order to take into account both zero values and protest answers in the model estimates (Strazzera et al. 2003; Grammatikopoulou and Olsen 2013). Glenk et al. (2012) argue that the latent class approach to modelling non-participation requires an absence of a priori assumptions about how to "treat" protest responses and serial non-participation, and has the advantage over alternative approaches such as double hurdle choice models (e.g. von Haefen et al. 2005) that it does not require a priori identification of non-participation (Burton and Rigby 2009). It is important to denote that identifying protest responses does not necessarily imply a binary (yes/no) treatment. Practitioners should always keep in mind that the way protesters are handled could significantly influence welfare measures.

Whether protest responses should be included or excluded from the data analysis remains an open question. While many applications tend to exclude them, others have argued that, in order to provide more conservative estimates of WTP, protest answers should be included in the data analysis (Carson and Hanemann 2005). As there is no agreement on the best treatment for protest responses, transparency both in detection and treatment of these responses is found to be essential (Johnston et al. 2017), especially if the DCE is conducted for policy purposes.

More specifically, practitioners should collect different reasons for opting-out or systematically choosing the status quo option, including both protest and other reasons, and comprehensively report on this matter, including the overall number of protesters (frequency and percentages), the method employed to determine them (open-ended versus attitudinal questions) and the influence on welfare estimates of including/excluding protest responses (Meyerhoff and Liebe 2010).

2.9 Identifying Strategic Bidders

Strategic behaviour occurs when respondents do not answer truthfully to the valuation questions of a survey because they think that they can affect the final outcome of the survey by answering differently (Hoyos and Mariel 2010). For example, they could answer affirmatively to a high price, showing that the good is very valuable although thinking that they will never have to pay it in reality. As seen in Sect. 2.4, this could be the case when the survey lacks incentive compatibility and payment consequentiality.

2.9 Identifying Strategic Bidders

Strategic behaviour from respondents has been used as a general criticism to mistrust SP survey responses, especially in the contingent valuation literature (Carson and Hanemann 2005; McFadden and Train 2017). However, strategic bias in empirical studies can be minimised through well-designed questionnaires (Mitchell and Carson 1989). For example, consistent with a lack of incentive compatibility and potentially inducing strategic behaviour, the use of open-ended questions in contingent valuation has decreased in recent years relative to other formats, in part due to the large number of respondents who provide either unrealistically high or zero WTP responses. Respondents with apparently extreme sensitivities can also be accommodated in discrete choice models (Campbell et al. 2010).

DCE have been found to help avoid strategic behaviour from the respondents (Hanley et al. 2001; Lancsar and Louviere 2008), although some authors like Day et al. (2012) find empirical evidence of strategic behaviour in the context of valuing public goods. Nonetheless, the researcher should bear in mind that the advanced disclosure of choice tasks often involved in a typical DCE as well as presenting multiple choice tasks and alternatives or even the order in which they are presented (i.e. departing from the theoretically incentive compatible single binary choice between the status quo and one alternative) could induce strategic behaviour from respondents (Collins and Vossler 2009; McNair et al. 2011; Vossler et al. 2012; Scheufele and Bennett 2012).

From the previous discussion, it is clearly unlikely that strategic responses will be avoided, so practitioners should try to minimise them by using incentive compatible choice experiments and plausible consequential decision setting while considering the use of other methods to minimise hypothetical bias.

2.10 Payment Vehicle and Cost Vector Design

The payment vehicle used can be anything from which respondents experience a negative utility (in a WTP setting, or a positive in a WTA setting). The crucial point is that it has to be considered realistic, relevant and consequential by the respondent. Thus, it relies heavily on the institutional context of a given country. In choosing the right payment vehicle, it is important to ensure a mandatory payment if used (see Sect. 2.5 on consequentiality), that it is a vehicle that is available to the respondents, and that the vehicle match the type of good. For example, if we are dealing with public good aspects of water, a water consumption user fee may lead to a high level of protesters, even if it is the only realistically available and mandatory payment vehicle (see Sect. 2.8). Hassan et al. (2018) have a thorough discussion of the choice of payment vehicle in a case where the choice was not so obvious.

The most common payment vehicles typically involve some kind of monetary transfer. Examples of payment vehicles in a utility enhancing context include income tax (Campbell et al. 2014), tax on water usage (Jørgensen et al. 2013), subsidy reduction (Hassan et al. 2018), entrance fee (Talpur et al. 2018), and in a utility decreasing context, subsidies paid to landowners (Vedel et al. 2015a), donations from NGOs (Rakotonarivo et al. 2017), lowering property tax (Vedel et al. 2015b), salaries from alternative employment (Nielsen et al. 2014), the opportunity gain of an interest free loan or labour (Kassahun and Jacobsen 2015). The choice of payment vehicle should always be guided and thoroughly tested in focus group interviews. In particular, it is important to ascertain that people consider the chosen payment vehicle to be both realistic, relevant and consequential for the specific valuation context.

Once the payment vehicle is decided on, an appropriate cost vector has to be determined. The lower bound of the cost vector will typically be logically located at zero if the survey aims at willingness-to-pay estimates. In the case of willingness to accept (WTA) estimates, of course, the cost levels might be negative indicating a discount, for example. Referring back to the dichotomous choice contingent valuation literature, greater effort is required to identify the upper end of the range. This is the so-called choke price, i.e. a payment level that is so high that it just chokes off (almost) any demand for the offered improvement—essentially the price at which the demand curve reaches zero. In the DCE context, this corresponds to a payment level at which almost no one (a commonly used rule of thumb is that it should be less than 5%) would choose the presented alternative regardless of the other attribute levels of the alternative and other available alternatives in the choice set. Once this upper bound of the cost vector has been found, a suitable number and location of levels needs to be set within the chosen lower and upper bound for the cost vector. Sufficiently high cost levels are particularly important for identifying respondents with a very low cost sensitivity who are typically situated in the tail of the distribution.

Concerning the number of levels of the cost attribute, narrowly focusing on D-efficiency is likely to lead to relatively few levels. Nevertheless, this may not be optimal given the importance of the estimated cost attribute parameter for the calculation of all WTP estimates. From this point of view, the cost parameter should be estimated with the highest possible precision, also for smaller level changes and to allow for possible nonlinear preferences. No fixed number of levels can be a priori recommended, but most practical applications of environmental DCE use more levels for the cost attribute than for non-cost attributes. Typically between 4 and 8 levels in addition to zero are used for the cost attribute. Next, the location of the levels within the range also needs to be determined. This could be done by distributing the levels evenly within the range. An example is the following cost vector with seven levels: {0; 10; 20; 30; 40; 50; 60}. Rather than using such equidistant spacing of levels in the cost vector, a more commonly used approach is to use (approximately) exponentially increasing distance between levels. An example using the same range as above is: {0; 2; 4; 8; 15; 30; 60}. However, to our knowledge no systematic investigation of the pros and cons of both approaches is available, as is also the problem for other aspects of the cost vector design mentioned above. When linear utility functions are used it may be beneficial to implement unequally spaced cost levels to increase the number of cost differences across the attributes, thereby facilitating the estimation of the cost coefficient, its heterogeneity and WTP measures accordingly.

Another decision to take is whether there should be non-status-quo alternatives with a price of zero. From a statistical point of view this may be wise, especially if the sign of some of the attributes may differ, but it may be problematic to ensure policy consequentiality if improvements can be obtained at no cost. Both approaches are found in the literature. In theory, the levels and range of the cost vector should not matter. The problem in a DCE context is, however, that there is evidence that people may anchor their choices in the payment levels and range presented (Glenk et al. 2019). For instance, Kragt (2013) analyses the importance of the bid range by a split sample where one split got a bid range from AU$ 0–400 and the other from AU$ 0–600, both with 5 levels in each. She concludes that respondents anchor their choices to relative bid levels; yet she finds little effect on the actual WTP. Other similar studies (e.g. Hanley et al. 2005; Carlsson and Martinsson 2008) find ambiguous evidence regarding impacts on WTP. More recently, Glenk et al. (2019) find WTP estimates to be significantly affected by the payment vector. Furthermore, Mørkbak et al. (2010) find that the specific choke price used may affect WTP estimates.

In conclusion, choosing the right payment vehicle is important to ensure consequentiality and thus validity of the study. It has to be broadly accepted in the population, mandatory for all to contribute to and there has to be trust in the institutional setting. This is typically identified and tested in focus groups, and further validated by follow-up questions after the choice sets in the survey. Despite the importance of the cost vector, there are few solid recommendations for determining an appropriate cost vector in practice—partly because it is highly context dependent. Identification of the cost vector should thus always be guided by inputs from focus group interviews. Furthermore, it should be ascertained in pilot tests that the cost attribute parameter can be estimated with a high level of statistical significance and that alternatives displaying the highest level of the cost vector are only very rarely chosen.

References

Aadland D, Caplan AJ (2003) Willingness to pay for curbside recycling with detection and mitigation of hypothetical bias. Am J Agr Econ 85:492–502. https://doi.org/10.1111/1467-8276.00136

Aadland D, Caplan AJ (2006) Cheap talk reconsidered: new evidence from CVM. J Econ Behav Organ 60:562–578. https://doi.org/10.1016/j.jebo.2004.09.006

Aanesen M, Armstrong C, Czajkowski M et al (2015) Willingness to pay for unfamiliar public goods: preserving cold-water coral in Norway. Ecol Econ 112:53–67. https://doi.org/10.1016/j.ecolecon.2015.02.007

Abate TG, Mørkbak MR, Olsen SB (2018) Inducing value and institutional learning effects in stated choice experiments using advanced disclosure and instructional choice set treatments. Agric Econ 49:339–351. https://doi.org/10.1111/agec.12420

Alemu MH, Olsen SB (2018) Can a repeated opt-out reminder mitigate hypothetical bias in discrete choice experiments? An application to consumer valuation of novel food products. Eur Rev Agric Econ 45:749–782. https://doi.org/10.1093/erae/jby009

Ami D, Aprahamian F, Chanel O, Luchini S (2011) A Test of cheap talk in different hypothetical contexts: the case of air pollution. Environ Resource Econ 50:111. https://doi.org/10.1007/s10640-011-9464-z

Andreoni J (1990) impure altruism and donations to public goods: a theory of warm-glow giving. Econ J 100:464–477. https://doi.org/10.2307/2234133

Arrow K, Solow R, Portney P et al (1993) Report of NOAA Panel on contingent valuation. Fed Reg 58:4601–4614

Barrage L, Lee MS (2010) A penny for your thoughts: inducing truth-telling in stated preference elicitation. Econ Lett 106:140–142. https://doi.org/10.1016/j.econlet.2009.11.006

Bateman IJ, Burgess D, Hutchinson WG, Matthews DI (2008) Learning design contingent valuation (LDCV): NOAA guidelines, preference learning and coherent arbitrariness. J Environ Econ Manag 55:127–141. https://doi.org/10.1016/j.jeem.2007.08.003

Bateman IJ, Carson RT, Day BH et al (2002) Economic valuation with stated preferences techniques: a manual. Edward Elgar, Cheltenham

Bateman IJ, Day BH, Jones AP, Jude S (2009) Reducing gain–loss asymmetry: a virtual reality choice experiment valuing land use change. J Environ Econ Manag 58:106–118. https://doi.org/10.1016/j.jeem.2008.05.003

Bishop RC, Boyle KJ, Carson RT et al (2017) Putting a value on injuries to natural assets: the BP oil spill. Science 356:253–254. https://doi.org/10.1126/science.aam8124

Bosworth R, Taylor LO (2012) Hypothetical bias in choice experiments: is cheap talk effective at eliminating bias on the intensive and extensive margins of choice? BE J Econ Anal Policy 12. https://doi.org/10.1515/1935-1682.3278

Bulte E, Gerking S, List JA, de Zeeuw A (2005) The effect of varying the causes of environmental problems on stated WTP values: evidence from a field study. J Environ Econ Manag 49:330–342. https://doi.org/10.1016/j.jeem.2004.06.001

Burton M, Rigby D (2009) Hurdle and latent class approaches to serial non-participation in choice models. Environ Resource Econ 42:211–226. https://doi.org/10.1007/s10640-008-9225-9

Campbell D, Hensher DA, Scarpa R (2014) Bounding WTP distributions to reflect the "actual" consideration set. J Choice Model 11:4–15. https://doi.org/10.1016/j.jocm.2014.02.004

Campbell D, Hess S, Scarpa R, Rose JM (2010) Accommodating coefficient outliers in discrete choice modelling: a comparison of discrete and continuous mixing approaches. In: Hess S, Daly A (eds) Choice modelling: The State-of-the-art and The State-of-practice. Emerald Group Publishing Limited, pp 331–352

Carlsson F, García JH, Löfgren Å (2010) Conformity and the demand for environmental goods. Environ Resource Econ 47:407–421. https://doi.org/10.1007/s10640-010-9385-2

Carlsson F, Kataria M, Krupnick A et al (2013) The truth, the whole truth, and nothing but the truth—a multiple country test of an oath script. J Econ Behav Organ 89:105–121. https://doi.org/10.1016/j.jebo.2013.02.003

Carlsson F, Martinsson P (2008) Does it matter when a power outage occurs?—a choice experiment study on the willingness to pay to avoid power outages. Energy Econ 30:1232–1245. https://doi.org/10.1016/j.eneco.2007.04.001

Carlsson F, Martinsson P, Akay A (2011) The effect of power outages and cheap talk on willingness to pay to reduce outages. Energy Econ 33:790–798. https://doi.org/10.1016/j.eneco.2011.01.004

Carlsson F, Mørkbak MR, Olsen SB (2012) The first time is the hardest: a test of ordering effects in choice experiments. J Choice Model 5:19–37. https://doi.org/10.1016/S1755-5345(13)70051-4

Carson RT (2000) Contingent valuation: a user's guide. Environ Sci Technol 34:1413–1418. https://doi.org/10.1021/es990728j

Carson RT, Groves T (2007) Incentive and informational properties of preference questions. Environ Resource Econ 37:181–210. https://doi.org/10.1007/s10640-007-9124-5

Carson RT, Groves T, List JA (2014) Consequentiality: a theoretical and experimental exploration of a single binary choice. J Assoc Environ Resource Econ 1:171–207. https://doi.org/10.1086/676450

Carson RT, Hanemann W (2005) Chapter 17 Contingent Valuation. Handbook of Environmental Economics 2:821–936. https://doi.org/10.1016/S1574-0099(05)02017-6

Champ PA, Moore R, Bishop RC (2009) A Comparison of approaches to mitigate hypothetical bias. Agric Resource Econ Rev 38:166–180. https://doi.org/10.1017/S106828050000318X

Carson RT, Louviere JJ, Anderson DA et al (1994) Experimental analysis of choice. Market Lett 5:351–367. https://doi.org/10.1007/BF00999210

Chilton SM, Hutchinson WG (1999) Do focus groups contribute anything to the contingent valuation process? J Econ Psychol 19

Collins JP, Vossler CA (2009) Incentive compatibility tests of choice experiment value elicitation questions. J Environ Econ Manag 58:226–235. https://doi.org/10.1016/j.jeem.2009.04.004

References

Cummings RG, Taylor LO (1999) Unbiased value estimates for environmental goods: a cheap talk design for the contingent valuation method. Am Econ Rev 89:649–665. https://doi.org/10.1257/aer.89.3.649

Day B, Bateman IJ, Carson RT et al (2012) Ordering effects and choice set awareness in repeat-response stated preference studies. J Environ Econ Manag 63:73–91. https://doi.org/10.1016/j.jeem.2011.09.001

de Magistris T, Gracia A, Nayga RM (2013) On the use of honesty priming tasks to mitigate hypothetical bias in choice experiments. Am J Agric Econ 95:1136–1154. https://doi.org/10.1093/ajae/aat052

de-Magistris T, Pascucci S (2014) The effect of the solemn oath script in hypothetical choice experiment survey: a pilot study. Economics Letters 123:252–255. https://doi.org/10.1016/j.econlet.2014.02.016

Dillman DA, Smyth JD, Christian LM (2008) Internet, mail, and mixed-mode Surveys: the tailored design method, 3rd Revised edn. Wiley, Hoboken, NJ

Dillman DA, Smyth JD, Christian LM (2014) Internet, mail, and mixed-mode surveys: the tailored design method, 4th edn. Wiley, Hoboken, NJ

Duncan GJ, Petersen E (2001) The long and short of asking questions about income, wealth, and labor supply. Soc Sci Res 30:248–263. https://doi.org/10.1006/ssre.2000.0696

Frey UJ, Pirscher F (2019) Distinguishing protest responses in contingent valuation: a conceptualization of motivations and attitudes behind them. PLoS ONE 14:e0209872. https://doi.org/10.1371/journal.pone.0209872

Galesic M, Bosnjak M (2009) Effects of questionnaire length on participation and indicators of response quality in a web survey. Public Opin Q 73:349–360. https://doi.org/10.1093/poq/nfp031

Glenk K, Colombo S (2011) How sure can you be? A framework for considering delivery uncertainty in benefit assessments based on stated preference methods. J Agric Econ 62:25–46. https://doi.org/10.1111/j.1477-9552.2010.00278.x

Glenk K, Hall C, Liebe U, Meyerhoff J (2012) Preferences of Scotch malt whisky consumers for changes in pesticide use and origin of barley. Food Policy 37:719–731. https://doi.org/10.1016/j.foodpol.2012.08.003

Glenk K, Meyerhoff J, Akaichi F, Martin-Ortega J (2019) Revisiting cost vector effects in discrete choice experiments. Resource Energy Econ 57:135–155. https://doi.org/10.1016/j.reseneeco.2019.05.001

Grammatikopoulou I, Olsen SB (2013) Accounting protesting and warm glow bidding in Contingent Valuation surveys considering the management of environmental goods—an empirical case study assessing the value of protecting a Natura 2000 wetland area in Greece. J Environ Manage 130:232–241. https://doi.org/10.1016/j.jenvman.2013.08.054

Groves RM, Presser S, Dipko S (2004) the role of topic interest in survey participation decisions. Public Opin Q 68:2–31. https://doi.org/10.1093/poq/nfh002

Hailu A, Adamowicz WL, Boxall PC (2000) Complements, substitutes, budget constraints and valuation: application of a multi-program environmental valuation method. Environ Resource Econ 16:51–68. https://doi.org/10.1023/A:1008328920083

Hanley N, Adamowicz W, Wright RE (2005) Price vector effects in choice experiments: an empirical test. Resource Energy Econ 27:227–234. https://doi.org/10.1016/j.reseneeco.2004.11.001

Hanley N, Mourato S, Wright RE (2001) Choice modelling approaches: a superior alternative for environmental valuation? J Econ Surv 15:435–462. https://doi.org/10.1111/1467-6419.00145

Hassan S, Olsen SB, Thorsen BJ (2019) Urban-rural divides in preferences for wetland conservation in Malaysia. Land Use Policy 84:226–237. https://doi.org/10.1016/j.landusepol.2019.03.015

Hassan S, Olsen SB, Thorsen BJ (2018) Appropriate payment vehicles in stated preference studies in developing economies. Environ Resource Econ 71:1053–1075. https://doi.org/10.1007/s10640-017-0196-6

Herriges J, Kling C, Liu C-C, Tobias J (2010) What are the consequences of consequentiality? J Environ Econ Manag 59:67–81. https://doi.org/10.1016/j.jeem.2009.03.004

Howard G, Roe BE, Nisbet EC, Martin J (2015) Hypothetical bias mitigation in choice experiments: effectiveness of cheap talk and honesty priming fade with repeated choices. Social Science Research Network, Rochester, NY

Hoyos D (2010) The state of the art of environmental valuation with discrete choice experiments. Ecol Econ 69:1595–1603. https://doi.org/10.1016/j.ecolecon.2010.04.011

Hoyos D, Mariel P (2010) Contingent valuation: past, present and future. Prague Economic Papers, 329–343. https://doi.org/10.18267/j.pep.380

Jacobsen JB, Boiesen JH, Thorsen BJ, Strange N (2008) What's in a name? The use of quantitative measures versus 'Iconised' species when valuing biodiversity. Environ Resource Econ 39:247–263. https://doi.org/10.1007/s10640-007-9107-6

Jacobsen JB, Lundhede TH, Martinsen L et al (2011) Embedding effects in choice experiment valuations of environmental preservation projects. Ecol Econ 70:1170–1177. https://doi.org/10.1016/j.ecolecon.2011.01.013

Jacquemet N, James A, Luchini S, Shogren JF (2017) Referenda under oath. Environ Resource Econ 67:479–504. https://doi.org/10.1007/s10640-016-0023-5

Jacquemet N, Joule R-V, Luchini S, Shogren JF (2013) Preference elicitation under oath. J Environ Econ Manag 65:110–132. https://doi.org/10.1016/j.jeem.2012.05.004

Jensen AK, Johnston RJ, Olsen SB (2019) Does one size really fit all? Ecological endpoint heterogeneity in stated preference welfare analysis. Land Econ 95:307–332. https://doi.org/10.3368/le.95.3.307

Johnston RJ, Boyle KJ, Adamowicz W (Vic) et al (2017) Contemporary guidance for stated preference studies. J Assoc Environ Resource Econ 4:319–405. https://doi.org/10.1086/691697

Jorgensen BS, Syme GJ (2000) Protest responses and willingness to pay: attitude toward paying for stormwater pollution abatement. Ecol Econ 33:251–265. https://doi.org/10.1016/S0921-8009(99)00145-7

Jørgensen SL, Olsen SB, Ladenburg J et al (2013) Spatially induced disparities in users' and non-users' WTP for water quality improvements—testing the effect of multiple substitutes and distance decay. Ecol Econ 92:58–66. https://doi.org/10.1016/j.ecolecon.2012.07.015

Kaplowitz MD, Hoehn JP (2001) Do focus groups and individual interviews reveal the same information for natural resource valuation? Ecol Econ 36:237–247. https://doi.org/10.1016/S0921-8009(00)00226-3

Kassahun HT, Jacobsen JB (2015) Economic and institutional incentives for managing the Ethiopian highlands of the Upper Blue Nile Basin: a latent class analysis. Land Use Policy 44:76–89. https://doi.org/10.1016/j.landusepol.2014.11.017

Kassahun HT, Nicholson CF, Jacobsen JB, Steenhuis TS (2016) Accounting for user expectations in the valuation of reliable irrigation water access in the Ethiopian highlands. Agric Water Manag 168:45–55. https://doi.org/10.1016/j.agwat.2016.01.017

Kragt ME (2013) The effects of changing cost vectors on choices and scale heterogeneity. Environ Resource Econ 54:201–221. https://doi.org/10.1007/s10640-012-9587-x

Krueger RA, Casey MA (2008) Focus Groups: a practical guide for applied research, 4th edn. Sage, Los Angeles

Ladenburg J, Dahlgaard JO, Bonnichsen O (2010) Testing the effect of a short cheap talk script in choice experiments. University of Copenhagen, Department of Food and Resource Economics

Ladenburg J, Olsen SB (2014) Augmenting short cheap talk scripts with a repeated opt-out reminder in choice experiment surveys. Resource Energy Econ 37:39–63. https://doi.org/10.1016/j.reseneeco.2014.05.002

Ladenburg J, Olsen SB (2008) Gender-specific starting point bias in choice experiments: evidence from an empirical study. J Environ Econ Manag 56:275–285. https://doi.org/10.1016/j.jeem.2008.01.004

Lancsar E, Louviere J (2008) Conducting discrete choice experiments to inform healthcare decision making: a user's guide. PharmacoEconomics 26:661–677. https://doi.org/10.2165/00019053-200826080-00004

References

Leeuw EDD, Hox J, Dillman D (2008) International handbook of survey methodology, 1st edn. Routledge, New York, London

Liebe U, Hundeshagen C, Beyer H, von Cramon-Taubadel S (2016) Context effects and the temporal stability of stated preferences. Soc Sci Res 60:135–147. https://doi.org/10.1016/j.ssresearch.2016.04.013

Lim SL, Yang J-C, Ehrisman J et al (2020) Are videos or text better for describing attributes in stated-preference surveys? Patient. https://doi.org/10.1007/s40271-020-00416-9

List JA (2001) Do explicit warnings eliminate the hypothetical bias in elicitation procedures? evidence from field auctions for sportscards. Am Econ Rev 91:1498–1507. https://doi.org/10.1257/aer.91.5.1498

List JA, Sinha P, Taylor MH (2006) Using choice experiments to value non-market goods and services: evidence from field experiments. BE J Econ Anal Policy 6. https://doi.org/10.2202/1538-0637.1132

Loomis J, Gonzalez-Caban A, Gregory R (1994) Do reminders of substitutes and budget constraints influence contingent valuation estimates? Land Econ 70:499–506. https://doi.org/10.2307/3146643

Lundhede T, Jacobsen JB, Hanley N et al (2015) Incorporating outcome uncertainty and prior outcome beliefs in stated preferences. Land Economics 91:296–316. https://doi.org/10.3368/le.91.2.296

Lusk JL (2003) Effects of cheap talk on consumer willingness-to-pay for golden rice. Am J Agric Econ 85:840–856. https://doi.org/10.1111/1467-8276.00492

Mahieu P-A (2010) Does gender matter when using cheap talk in contingent valuation studies? Econ Bull 30:2955–2961

Matthews Y, Scarpa R, Marsh D (2017) Using virtual environments to improve the realism of choice experiments: A case study about coastal erosion management. J Environ Econ Manag 81:193–208. https://doi.org/10.1016/j.jeem.2016.08.001

McFadden D, Train K (2017) Contingent valuation of environmental goods: a comprehensive critique. Edward Elgar Publishing

McNair BJ, Bennett J, Hensher DA, Rose JM (2011) Households' willingness to pay for overhead-to-underground conversion of electricity distribution networks. Energy Policy 39:2560–2567. https://doi.org/10.1016/j.enpol.2011.02.023

Meyerhoff J, Bartczak A, Liebe U (2012) Protester or non-protester: a binary state? On the use (and non-use) of latent class models to analyse protesting in economic valuation. Aust J Agric Resource Econ 56:438–454. https://doi.org/10.1111/j.1467-8489.2012.00582.x

Meyerhoff J, Glenk K (2015) Learning how to choose-effects of instructional choice sets in discrete choice experiments. Resource Energy Econ 41:122–142. https://doi.org/10.1016/j.reseneeco.2015.04.006

Meyerhoff J, Liebe U (2006) Protest beliefs in contingent valuation: explaining their motivation. Ecol Econ 57:583–594. https://doi.org/10.1016/j.ecolecon.2005.04.021

Meyerhoff J, Liebe U (2010) Determinants of protest responses in environmental valuation: a meta-study. Ecol Econ 70:366–374. https://doi.org/10.1016/j.ecolecon.2010.09.008

Mitchell RC, Carson RT (1989) Using surveys to value public goods: the contingent valuation method. RFF Press, Washington, D.C.

Moore DW (2002) Measuring new types of question-order effects: additive and subtractive. Public Opin Q 66:80–91. https://doi.org/10.1086/338631

Morgan DL (1997) Focus groups as qualitative research, 1st edn. Sage, Thousand Oaks, CA

Mørkbak MR, Christensen T, Gyrd-Hansen D (2010) Choke price bias in choice experiments. Environ Resource Econ 45:537–551. https://doi.org/10.1007/s10640-009-9327-z

Morrison M, Brown TC (2009) Testing the effectiveness of certainty scales, cheap talk, and dissonance-minimization in reducing hypothetical bias in contingent valuation studies. Environ Resource Econ 44:307–326. https://doi.org/10.1007/s10640-009-9287-3

Moser R, Raffaelli R, Notaro S (2014) Testing hypothetical bias with a real choice experiment using respondents' own money. Eur Rev Agric Econ 41:25–46. https://doi.org/10.1093/erae/jbt016

Murphy JJ, Allen PG, Stevens TH, Weatherhead D (2005) A meta-analysis of hypothetical bias in stated preference valuation. Environ Resource Econ 30:313–325

Nayga RM, Woodward R, Aiew W (2006) Willingness to pay for reduced risk of foodborne illness: a nonhypothetical field experiment. Can J Agric Econ/Revue Canadienne D'agroeconomie 54:461–475. https://doi.org/10.1111/j.1744-7976.2006.00061.x

Nielsen ASE, Lundhede TH, Jacobsen JB (2016) Local consequences of national policies—a spatial analysis of preferences for forest access reduction. Forest Policy Econ 73:68–77. https://doi.org/10.1016/j.forpol.2016.08.010

Nielsen MR, Jacobsen JB, Thorsen BJ (2014) Factors determining the choice of hunting and trading bushmeat in the Kilombero Valley, Tanzania. Conserv Biol 28:382–391. https://doi.org/10.1111/cobi.12197

Oehlmann M, Meyerhoff J (2017) Stated preferences towards renewable energy alternatives in Germany—do the consequentiality of the survey and trust in institutions matter? J Environ Econ Policy 6:1–16. https://doi.org/10.1080/21606544.2016.1139468

Ozdemir S, Johnson FR, Hauber AB (2009) Hypothetical bias, cheap talk, and stated willingness to pay for health care. J Health Econ 28:894–901. https://doi.org/10.1016/j.jhealeco.2009.04.004

Palm-Forster LH, Ferraro PJ, Janusch N et al (2019) Behavioral and experimental agri-environmental research: methodological challenges, literature gaps, and recommendations. Environ Resource Econ 73:719–742. https://doi.org/10.1007/s10640-019-00342-x

Patterson Z, Darbani JM, Rezaei A et al (2017) Comparing text-only and virtual reality discrete choice experiments of neighbourhood choice. Landscape Urban Plan 157:63–74. https://doi.org/10.1016/j.landurbplan.2016.05.024

Pouta E (2004) Attitude and belief questions as a source of context effect in a contingent valuation survey. J Econ Psychol 25:229–242. https://doi.org/10.1016/S0167-4870(02)00170-8

Rakotonarivo OS, Jacobsen JB, Larsen HO et al (2017) Qualitative and quantitative evidence on the true local welfare costs of forest conservation in Madagascar: are discrete choice experiments a valid ex ante tool? World Dev 94:478–491. https://doi.org/10.1016/j.worlddev.2017.02.009

Rid W, Haider W, Ryffel A, Beardmore B (2018) Visualisations in choice experiments: comparing 3D film-sequences and still-images to analyse housing development alternatives. Ecol Econ 146:203–217. https://doi.org/10.1016/j.ecolecon.2017.10.019

Rolfe J, Bennett J, Louviere J (2002) Stated values and reminders of substitute goods: testing for framing effects with choice modelling. Aust J Agric Resource Econ 46:1–20. https://doi.org/10.1111/1467-8489.00164

Rossetti T, Hurtubia R (2020) An assessment of the ecological validity of immersive videos in stated preference surveys. J Choice Model 34:100198. https://doi.org/10.1016/j.jocm.2019.100198

Sandorf ED, Aanesen M, Navrud S (2016) Valuing unfamiliar and complex environmental goods: a comparison of valuation workshops and internet panel surveys with videos. Ecol Econ 129:50–61. https://doi.org/10.1016/j.ecolecon.2016.06.008

Scheufele G, Bennett J (2012) Response strategies and learning in discrete choice experiments. Environ Resource Econ 52:435–453. https://doi.org/10.1007/s10640-011-9537-z

Schkade DA, Payne JW (1994) How people respond to contingent valuation questions: a verbal protocol analysis of willingness to pay for an environmental regulation. J Environ Econ Manag 26:88–109. https://doi.org/10.1006/jeem.1994.1006

Schuman H, Presser S, Ludwig J (1981) Context effects on survey responses to questions about abortion. Public Opin Q 45:216–223. https://doi.org/10.1086/268652

Silva A, Nayga RM, Campbell BL, Park JL (2011) Revisiting cheap talk with new evidence from a field experiment. J Agric Resource Econ 36:280–291. https://doi.org/10.22004/ag.econ.117168

Stevens TH, Tabatabaei M, Lass D (2013) Oaths and hypothetical bias. J Environ Manage 127:135–141. https://doi.org/10.1016/j.jenvman.2013.04.038

Strange N, Jacobsen JB, Thorsen BJ, Tarp P (2007) Value for money: protecting endangered species on Danish Heathland. Environ Manage 40:761–774. https://doi.org/10.1007/s00267-006-0221-y

Strazzera E, Genius M, Scarpa R, Hutchinson G (2003) The effect of protest votes on the estimates of wtp for use values of recreational sites. Environ Resource Econ 25:461–476. https://doi.org/10.1023/A:1025098431440

References

Svenningsen LS (2019) Social preferences for distributive outcomes of climate policy. Climatic Change 157:319–336. https://doi.org/10.1007/s10584-019-02546-y

Talpur MA, Koetse MJ, Brouwer R (2018) Accounting for implicit and explicit payment vehicles in a discrete choice experiment. J Environ Econ Policy 7:363–385. https://doi.org/10.1080/21606544.2018.1450789

Tonsor GT, Shupp RS (2011) cheap talk scripts and online choice experiments: "looking beyond the mean." Am J Agric Econ 93:1015–1031. https://doi.org/10.1093/ajae/aar036

Tourangeau R, Rasinski KA (1988) Cognitive processes underlying context effects in attitude measurement. Psychol Bull 103:299–314. https://doi.org/10.1037/0033-2909.103.3.299

Tourangeau R, Rips LJ, Rasinski K (2000) The psychology of survey response. Cambridge University Press, New York

Uggeldahl KC (2018) Essays on decision making processes, information acquisition, and preferences in stated choice experiments: applications to economic valuation of consumer and environmental goods. https://ifro.ku.dk/english/research/past_phd_defences/2018/phd-23-august-2018/. Accessed 12 Aug 2019

Varela E, Mahieu P-A, Giergiczny M et al (2014) Testing the single opt-out reminder in choice experiments: an application to fuel break management in Spain. J Forest Econ 20:212–222. https://doi.org/10.1016/j.jfe.2014.05.001

Vedel SE, Jacobsen JB, Thorsen BJ (2015a) Contracts for afforestation and the role of monitoring for landowners' willingness to accept. Forest Policy Econ 51:29–37. https://doi.org/10.1016/j.forpol.2014.11.007

Vedel SE, Jacobsen JB, Thorsen BJ (2015b) Forest owners' willingness to accept contracts for ecosystem service provision is sensitive to additionality. Ecol Econ 113:15–24. https://doi.org/10.1016/j.ecolecon.2015.02.014

Von Haefen RH, Massey DM, Adamowicz WL (2005) Serial nonpanticipation in repeated discrete choice models. Am J Agr Econ 87:1061–1076. https://doi.org/10.1111/j.1467-8276.2005.00794.x

Vossler CA, Doyon M, Rondeau D (2012) Truth in consequentiality: theory and field evidence on discrete choice experiments. Am Econ J Microecon 4:145–171. https://doi.org/10.1257/mic.4.4.145

Vossler CA, Evans MF (2009) Bridging the gap between the field and the lab: environmental goods, policy maker input, and consequentiality. J Environ Econ Manag 58:338–345. https://doi.org/10.1016/j.jeem.2009.04.007

Vossler CA, Zawojska E (2020) Behavioral drivers or economic incentives? Toward a better understanding of elicitation effects in stated preference studies. J Assoc Environ Resource Econ 7:279–303. https://doi.org/10.1086/706645

Whitehead JC, Blomquist GC (1999) Do reminders of substitutes and budget constraints influence contingent valuation estimates? Reply to another comment. Land Economics 75:483–484. https://doi.org/10.2307/3147193

Willis GB (2005) Cognitive interviewing: a tool for improving questionnaire design. Sage, Thousand Oaks, CA

Wright JD, Marsden PV (eds) (2010) Handbook of survey research, 2nd Revised. Emerald Group Publishing, West Yorkshire, England

Zawojska E, Bartczak A, Czajkowski M (2019) Disentangling the effects of policy and payment consequentiality and risk attitudes on stated preferences. J Environ Econ Manag 93:63–84. https://doi.org/10.1016/j.jeem.2018.11.007

Zawojska E, Czajkowski M (2017) Re-examining empirical evidence on stated preferences: importance of incentive compatibility. J Environ Econ Policy 6:374–403. https://doi.org/10.1080/21606544.2017.1322537

Zillmann D, Schmitz A, Skopek J, Blossfeld H-P (2014) Survey topic and unit nonresponse. Qual Quant 48:2069–2088. https://doi.org/10.1007/s11135-013-9880-y

Open Access This chapter is licensed under the terms of the Creative Commons Attribution 4.0 International License (http://creativecommons.org/licenses/by/4.0/), which permits use, sharing, adaptation, distribution and reproduction in any medium or format, as long as you give appropriate credit to the original author(s) and the source, provide a link to the Creative Commons license and indicate if changes were made.

The images or other third party material in this chapter are included in the chapter's Creative Commons license, unless indicated otherwise in a credit line to the material. If material is not included in the chapter's Creative Commons license and your intended use is not permitted by statutory regulation or exceeds the permitted use, you will need to obtain permission directly from the copyright holder.

Chapter 3
Experimental Design

Abstract This chapter covers various issues related to the experimental design, a statistical technique at the core of a discrete choice experiment. Specifically, it focuses on the dimensionality of a choice experiment and the statistical techniques used to allocate attribute levels to choice tasks. Among others, the pros and cons of orthogonal designs, optimal orthogonal in the differences designs as well as efficient designs are addressed. The last section shows how a simulation exercise can help to test the appropriateness of the experimental design.

3.1 The Dimensionality of a Choice Experiment

The following five features can characterise the dimensionality of a choice experiment: the number of attributes, the number of levels used to describe the corresponding attribute, the range of the attribute levels, the number of alternatives presented in a choice task and, finally, the number of choice tasks. Considering the dimensions of a DCE is important as trade-offs might exist between their size and what is referred to as response efficiency. Response efficiency, according to Johnson et al. (2013, p. 6), refers to "measurement error resulting from respondents' inattention to the choice questions or other unobserved, contextual influences". Therefore, a low response efficiency means that respondents are less likely to identify the alternatives they prefer the most and will reduce choice consistency, i.e. the unexplained part or error term will vary to a greater extent. However, this effect does not take place uniformly for all design dimensions as the literature shows.

Two studies so far have systematically investigated the influence of all five dimensions on respondents' choices: Caussade et al. (2005) in transportation and Meyerhoff et al. (2015), building on Caussade et al. (2005) and Hensher (2006), in environmental economics. Both studies have used a so-called design-of-designs approach. Other important studies on this topic have been conducted by DeShazo and Fermo (2002), Boxall et al. (2009), Boyle and Özdemir (2009), Rolfe and Bennett (2009), Zhang and Adamowicz (2011), Hess et al. (2012), Czajkowski et al. (2014), and Campbell et al. (2015). Below we look at the various design dimensions separately.

3.1.1 Number of Choice Tasks

People responsible for designing a DCE are often afraid of presenting respondents with too many choice tasks. There are several published papers where it is suggested that presenting respondents "with more than four or six choice tasks" would be too much for them as it would be too complex and respondents would tire when having to respond to numerous tasks. However, the literature does not support this idea. There is, of course, a maximum number of choice tasks an individual is able (and willing) to respond to, but the number of tasks that respondents can answer before becoming fatigued seems to be higher than is often assumed. Hess et al. (2012), investigating different data sets from choice experiments conducted in transportation, argue that concerns about fatigue are probably overstated. Accommodating for scale heterogeneity had little or no impact on substantive models results, and the role of the constants in the models generally decreased. Czajkowski et al. (2014), for example, presented respondents with 26 choice tasks and were not able to identify clear signs of fatigue. Meyerhoff et al. (2015) were also not able to conclude that respondents who faced numerous choice tasks were significantly more likely to drop out of the survey. They presented splits of respondents in their design-of-designs approach with 6, 12, 18 and 24 choice tasks. Also Campbell et al. (2015) could not find strong evidence for fatigue in their study either, respondents were asked to respond to 16 choice tasks. Presenting more choice tasks than originally thought is therefore an option to be considered.

Moreover, a higher number of choice tasks is also crucial when calculating individual-specific WTP values as these conditional values are only meaningful when a sufficient number of choices is available for each respondent (Train 2009, Chap. 11; Sarrias 2020). However, further research would be helpful as the present findings might depend on the specific study contexts or on survey mode. Responding to 16 choice tasks in an online survey might, for example, be different from responding to 16 choice tasks in a paper and pencil survey. In any case, it is important to test prior to the survey whether the intended number of choice tasks can be considered manageable for the average respondent.

3.1.2 Number of Attributes

The studies by Caussade et al. (2005) and Meyerhoff et al. (2015) also suggest that increasing the number of attributes does not affect response efficiency negatively. Caussade et al. (2005) varied the number of attributes from 3 to 6, while Meyerhoff et al. (2015) varied them from 4 to 7. However, both expanded the number of attributes without adding new content. Caussade et al. (2005) presented to a split sample, for example, the attributes "free flow time" and "congestion time" instead of the attribute "total travel time" to increase the number of attributes. Meyerhoff et al. (2015) increased the number of attributes by splitting the attribute "overall biodiversity"

3.1 The Dimensionality of a Choice Experiment   39

into "biodiversity in forests" and "biodiversity in other parts of the landscape", for instance. Thus, it is not clear from either study whether this approach of expanding attributes is the reason why negative effects are not found with a higher number of attributes. Outcomes might be different when each attribute introduces a new characteristic of the good in question and therefore would clearly increase the amount of information a respondent would have to process. For the selection of attributes, see also Greiner et al. (2014).

3.1.3 Number of Alternatives

A dimension that might be more critical in terms of negative impacts on response efficiency is probably the number of alternatives. Findings by Zhang and Adamowicz (2011) suggest that with a larger number of alternatives the complexity increases. They compared choice tasks with two and choice tasks with three alternatives. They also point out that the increase in complexity might outweigh the benefits from the fact that people who are presented with more alternatives are more likely to find the alternative that matches their preferences best. Boyle and Özdemir (2009) find that respondents were more likely to choose the status quo (SQ) alternative when there were three alternatives on a choice task compared to tasks with two alternatives. This finding is supported by Oehlmann et al. (2017) who found that the number of alternatives has a significant impact on the frequency of status quo choices, i.e. the alternative with a zero price offer describing the current situation. The more alternatives a choice task comprised, the less often the status quo alternative was chosen.

A processing strategy that might be triggered by the number of alternatives is a switch from comparing the overall utility of an alternative to using the levels of the cost attribute as an indicator of quality alone. Meyerhoff et al. (2017) compared the effects of varying the number of choice tasks by comparing results from split samples where respondents faced different numbers of alternatives. In the splits with four and five alternatives, in addition to the status quo alternative, people seem to be more likely to switch to cost as an indicator of quality. In contrast, Czajkowski et al. (2014) observed no differences to WTP estimates when comparing choice tasks with two and three alternatives.

3.1.4 Other Dimensionality Issues

The number of attribute levels and the value range of the levels can have a positive effect on response efficiency and thus, choice consistency but also in identifying potential non-linear relationships for a given attribute. In line with the findings by Caussade et al. (2005), Meyerhoff et al. (2015) found that a higher number of attribute levels seems to impact on choice consistency positively, as does a narrow range of the level values. In both cases, it is probably easier for respondents to identify the preferred alternative when comparing the set of alternatives presented on a choice task. Also a higher number of attribute levels also makes a level balanced design more likely (see Sect. 3.2).

Another important point to consider is the randomisation of the order of appearance of the choice tasks if the survey mode allows for this to reduce the impact of anchoring (Jacobsen and Thorsen 2010) and to accommodate for scale heterogeneity (see Sect. 6.2). Also note that respondents might react differently to a long sequence of tasks in an online survey compared to a paper and pencil survey, so knowing the survey mode when deciding on the design dimensions is beneficial.

Regarding attribute non-attendance (Sect. 6.5), Weller et al. (2014) investigated whether stated or inferred attribute non-attendance are linked to the dimensions of the DCE. Overall, their results indicated only a weak relationship between attribute non-attendance and the design dimensions. They suggest, however, that a higher degree of non-attendance might take place when the number of alternatives and choice sets increases; more evidence is needed to draw stronger conclusions here.

A recommendation made by Zhang and Adamowicz (2011) is supported here. If you can afford another split in your survey design, you may consider employing choice tasks with only two alternatives that are said to perform better concerning incentive compatibility (see Sect. 2.4). Splits with choice tasks with two alternatives provide a yardstick for judging the effects of choice task with more alternatives. Also, if the sample is large enough and the order of appearance is randomised, it is possible to estimate simple models such as the conditional logit using only the responses to the first choice task each respondent faced while checking for potential differences.

An issue that requires further research is the relationship between dimensionality and incentive compatibility (see also Sect. 2.4). Generally, binary choices are seen as incentive compatible, i.e., respondents to this format should theoretically reveal true preferences. Whether this also applies to (a) a sequence of tasks with two alternatives, and (b) to sequences of choice tasks with more than two alternatives is still an open question. Vossler et al. (2012) show that under certain conditions, sequences of binary choice questions are incentive compatible but additional work on the association between the dimensionality of a choice experiment and incentive compatibility would be well received.

3.2 Statistical Design of the Choice Tasks

The purpose of an SP study is to learn about individual preferences. The benefit of using an SP survey is that, in contrast to RP, we can control the choices we present to people. In designing these choice tasks, two criteria are of importance. First, the choices presented to respondents need to be relevant. Second, the informational content (from a statistical point of view) of the design needs to be maximised. We need to present respondents with the trade-offs that provide us the best possible information about the preferences in the sample of interest (i.e. the coefficients of the utility function). Below, it is assumed that the attributes and the relevant levels are given and have been defined in a stage prior to the experimental design.

Originally, orthogonal designs were applied in DCE. Orthogonal designs ensure that the attribute levels are independent of each other, i.e. have zero correlation. In linear economic models, such as the linear regression model, orthogonal designs are also optimal from a statistical point of view. However, when working with discrete choice models, which are highly non-linear, this equivalence no longer holds. It is important to note that the underlying utility functions may be linear-in-parameters, but the choice probabilities are highly non-linear. A benefit of orthogonal designs is that they remove the correlation across key attributes of interest and thereby allow easy identification of their influence on utility. Moreover, orthogonal designs ensure that (i) every pair of attribute levels appears equally often across all pairs of alternatives and (ii) attribute levels are balanced, i.e. each level occurs the same number of times for each alternative.

Orthogonality, however, does not consider the realism of the choice tasks and often the design includes alternatives that are dominated (e.g. both worse in quality and more expensive). Also, random and orthogonal designs are more robust across modelling assumptions but inherently result in a loss of efficiency (Yao et al. 2015). Hence, alternative design generation strategies were being formulated. One of these strategies is Optimal Orthogonal in the Differences (OOD) designs as introduced by Street et al. (2001, 2005). These *D-optimal* designs still maintain orthogonality, but attributes that are common across alternatives are not allowed to take the same level in the design, hence the term *optimal in the differences*. The Ngene manual (ChoiceMetrics 2018) highlights that OOD designs can only be used for unlabelled experiments and may stimulate certain types of behaviour since specific attributes may influence the entire experiment given that the levels are never the same across alternatives. Due to this nature of OOD designs, efficient designs have developed as a popular alternative. By optimising for a specific utility function, we obtain more information about the parameters of interest from the same amount of choices.

More information typically means obtaining more efficient parameter estimates and generally that implies lower standard errors. However, the efficient design literature makes use of alternative efficiency definitions. That is, different definitions of efficiency have an objective that goes beyond reducing the standard error of the parameter estimates. To make this clearer, we need to trace back to the origin of the standard errors. They are generally obtained from the Hessian (i.e. the matrix of second-order derivatives of the log-likelihood function) evaluated at the estimated values of the parameters. The Hessian summarises all the uncertainty associated with the parameters of interest. The negative inverse of this matrix is also known as the asymptotic covariance (AVC) matrix of parameter estimates and the square root of the diagonal terms gives us our standard errors of interest. The off-diagonal elements capture the extent to which alternative parameters can be identified independently from each other. The latter is crucial information since reducing the standard error on one parameter may mean we may no longer be able to separate that specific effect from other attributes in the SP study.

In short, we want to minimise the uncertainty, or maximise the informational content, in our experiment as summarised by the Fisher information matrix. Maximising something, however, requires a unique number and not a matrix. Hence, we need to reduce the dimensionality of the Hessian to a single number and that is where the efficient design *alphabet soup* comes into play (Olsen and Meyerhoff 2017).

The most widely used efficiency measure is the D-error, where alternative designs are compared based on the determinant of the AVC matrix. A D-efficient design is the design that has a sufficiently low D-error. Note that it is often impossible to find the D-optimal design, which has the lowest possible D-error, due to the large number of possible design combinations. By focusing on the determinant, it does not solely focus on minimising the standard errors, but also takes into account the degree of correlation between parameters. The D-error can also be directly related to the measure of information in the Fisher information matrix through the eigenvectors, hence explaining the popularity of this measure. Software packages, such as Ngene (ChoiceMetrics 2018), also allow us to find efficient designs using alternative efficiency measures:

(a) A-efficiency: this efficiency measure minimises the trace of the AVC matrix and thereby only looks at the variances (standard errors) and not the covariances between parameters estimates. It is important for this measure to work effectively that all parameters are of comparable scale.

(b) C-efficiency: this efficiency measure works particularly well when interested in WTP measures since it focuses on minimising the variances (standard errors) of parameter ratios.

(c) D-efficiency minimises the determinant of the Hessian. Thus, it tries to minimise the standard errors on the diagonal, while at the same time controlling for the degree of correlation between parameter estimates. The D-efficiency criterion is the most commonly used criterion in the literature.

(d) S-efficiency: this efficiency criterion finds its origin in the t-value (ratio of the parameter over its standard error). It aims to identify the number of repetitions in the design that are needed for a parameter to be significant. S-efficient designs spread the amount of information across the parameters of interest and hence minimises the number of repetitions needed to obtain significant parameter estimates for all parameters. The S-statistic is merely a lower bound, since the optimisation assumes that respondents act according to the specified prior parameter values.

An detailed description of the alternative design measures and the theory of efficient design is given in the Ngene manual (ChoiceMetrics 2018). It should be noted that all efficiency criteria make use of the AVC matrix, which inherently depends on the parameters of the model. More explicitly, the AVC matrix of the multinomial logit (MNL) model is a function of the parameters of the model. This explains the requirement of efficient designs to define prior parameter values when generating the design. As such, the design will be optimised for these specific parameter values and is therefore optimised locally. If preferences in society differ, it is therefore

3.2 Statistical Design of the Choice Tasks

not guaranteed that this will be the best design. Alternative strategies can therefore be employed. First, it is always good practice to base prior parameters on existing values in the literature. Second, it is also common practice to generate an initial design based on non-efficient design criteria (random designs, or orthogonal designs). This non-optimal design then serves as the basis in a pre-test from which a set of prior values can then be elicited. However, it needs to be ensured that the sample size of the pre-test is sufficiently large to make useful inferences about the parameters of interest.

Even after employing these strategies, the researcher is typically left with a significant degree of uncertainty about the parameters of interest. To optimise the design over a larger region of parameter estimates one typically reverts to Bayesian designs. The terminology for Bayesian designs is rather unfortunate, since the design criterion is still based on the AVC matrix which plays no role of interest in Bayesian estimation. Nevertheless, the terminology does capture that the parameters of interest are inherently uncertain. The researcher is therefore requested to specify a prior density (e.g. normal or uniform distribution) describing the possible range and likelihood for the potential parameter values (Bliemer and Collins 2016). The design generation then optimises the design by taking a weighted average of the design criterion over all possible parameter values. A direct result of optimising over a wider range of parameter values is that the design is more generic and is thereby likely to lose some efficiency. However, this would only be the case when we accurately know our parameters of interest. Bayesian designs can therefore be labelled as good practice. A general guideline here is that the less known about the parameter estimates of interest, the wider the range should be of parameter values specified for the Bayesian design to reflect this uncertainty.

The AVC matrix does not only depend on the parameters of interest, but also on our assumption about the error term and the functional form of the utility function. Van Cranenburgh et al. (2018), for example, illustrate that designs generated for a RUM decision criterion may not be overly suited to identify choices based on a Random Regret Minimisation (RRM) decision rule. Similarly, Ngene (ChoiceMetrics 2018) allows us to generate designs for non-MNL models, such as nested logit and MXL. Indeed, such models are associated with a much more complicated likelihood function and thus a definition of the Hessian, but the underlying principles of generating efficient designs are not affected. The challenge, however, is that a priori we typically do not know which models we will estimate. Moreover, unlike Bayesian efficient designs, there are currently no design algorithms that allow optimisation of the design over a range of model specifications. As such, it is good practice to generate the design for the most generic model possible (typically the MXL). Generating mixed logit designs takes much longer and is therefore often avoided despite being good practice. An alternative is again to use random or orthogonal designs which are more robust across modelling assumptions but inherently result in a loss of efficiency. In the end, the researcher should be reminded that variations in the attribute levels is of most importance and that efficient designs are only aimed at obtaining more information from the same amount of choices *for a set of given modelling assumptions*.

Recently, the focus in the literature has been on the generation of efficient designs. Statistical efficiency is, however, not the panacea and only criteria that determine the quality of the design. An efficient design is optimised for a given model and there are numerous reasons why that model may be misspecified and hence it would not be appropriate to characterise the response behaviour. Accordingly, it is considered good practice to have a larger number of choice tasks to better cover the space of potential attribute level combinations.

Finally, most experimental designs are only based on main effects and do not consider interaction effects between parameters. As an analyst, when we wish to learn about two-way interaction effects (i.e. how combinations of attributes and their levels influence utility) this requires presenting specific combinations of attribute levels. These requirements can be accommodated in both orthogonal and efficient designs relatively easily. However, to empirically identify interaction effects typically significantly larger sample sizes are required as opposed to identifying main effects. To see this, one can easily compare the S-efficiency statistic across designs (not) including interaction effects.

In summary, practitioners should bear in mind that the key to obtaining informative results is presenting respondents with different trade-offs. Hence, the more attribute levels and the more choice tasks the better. Using blocking across respondents to obtain more versions of the design to learn more about preferences across respondents may also be recommended. Alternatively, tasks can be randomly assigned to respondents, especially when the overall number of choice tasks is rather large. Also, when developing surveys start off with simple orthogonal designs or random designs and use the result from the pilot for updating the priors. Finally, convention so far states that MNL-based efficient designs perform well and not much worse compared to the designs optimised for more advanced models (Bliemer and Rose 2010, 2011).

3.3 Checking Your Statistical Design

The so-called right-hand side matrix in a linear regression is formed by the explanatory variables. In a discrete choice model, this matrix is defined by the variables included in V_{njt} in Eq. (1.3) that can be alternative specific constants, attributes, individual-specific variables or their interactions. The right-hand side matrix of discrete choice models plays a crucial role in parameter identification and the precision of their estimation. As described above, the right-hand side matrix in SP data sets is usually set by the experimental design. A high number of attributes, and/or attribute levels, can make the search for a convenient experimental design a tricky task. The literature on experimental designs (Street and Burgess 2007; Louviere and Lancsar 2009; ChoiceMetrics 2018) describes how to generate them, how to analyse their properties and efficiency or how to block them. Nevertheless, in the applied literature, not sufficient attention is usually paid to all these steps and they are usually not sufficiently described. Moreover, sometimes the coding used in the experimental design has been changed in the econometric analysis. For example, efficient designs

3.3 Checking Your Statistical Design

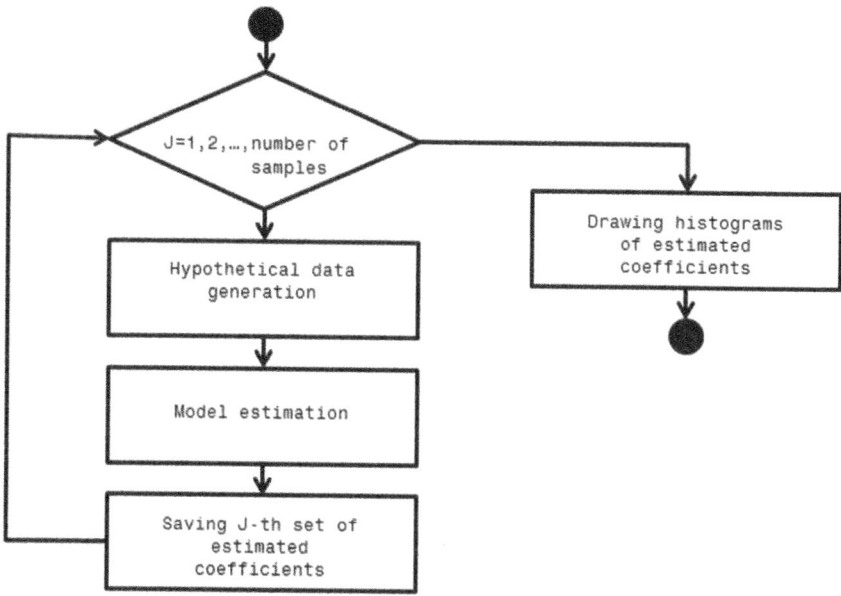

Fig. 3.1 Flowchart of a simulation exercise

with attribute levels specified as continuous (e.g. 1, 2, 3, 4) are coded as categorical after the data were collected. This categorical coding can be inappropriate for parameter identification.

The appropriateness of an experimental design or, generally speaking, the appropriateness of the right-hand side matrix of discrete choice models can be easily checked by a simulation exercise presented in Fig. 3.1.

This check is based on the generation of numerous hypothetical data sets based on the generated (SP data) or collected (revealed preference (RP) data) right-hand side matrix. The hypothetical data sets are generated by setting the values of the parameters to a specific value assuming that these are the true population values and generating specific values of the error components. In each iteration, a hypothetical data set is used for a model estimation and the set of estimated parameters is saved.

Post-analysis of the empirical distribution of all parameters can reveal whether the right-hand side matrix allows for an unbiased estimation of all the parameters, as the true population parameters are known. This simple simulation exercise should always be carried out both in RP and in SP studies. In RP studies, it allows us to check whether the variation of the collected attribute levels is sufficient to identify all the parameters correctly. In SP studies, it allows us to check the appropriateness of the generated experimental design as well as the expected distribution of the parameter estimates.

For example, imagine we want to analyse the appropriateness of the following experimental design

alt1.attr1	alt1.attr2	alt2.attr1	alt2.attr2	alt3.attr1	alt3.attr2
1	3	3	5	9	9
7	1	7	7	5	5
7	9	5	1	5	9
1	3	9	1	7	7
5	9	3	9	7	1
9	5	1	7	1	3
3	7	9	3	1	5
5	1	7	9	3	3
9	7	1	3	3	7
3	5	5	5	9	1

corresponding to a one choice-occasion with three alternatives and two attributes defined according to the Eq. (1.4), as

$$U_{n1} = ASC_1 + \beta_1 \text{attr}_{n1} + \beta_2 \text{attr}_{n2} + \varepsilon_{n1}$$
$$U_{n2} = ASC_2 + \beta_1 \text{attr}_{n2} + \beta_2 \text{attr}_{n2} + \varepsilon_{n2}$$
$$U_{n3} = \beta_1 \text{attr}_{n3} + \beta_2 \text{attr}_{n3} + \varepsilon_{n3}$$

Subsequently, we assume that the following values of the parameters are population values

$$U_{n1} = 0.5 + 0.1 \text{ attr}_{n1} - 0.1 \text{ attr}_{n2} + \varepsilon_{n1}$$
$$U_{n2} = 0.5 + 0.1 \text{ attr}_{n2} - 0.1 \text{ attr}_{n2} + \varepsilon_{n2}$$
$$U_{n3} = 0.1 \text{ attr}_{n3} - 0.1 \text{ attr}_{n3} + \varepsilon_{n3}$$

and generate, for example, 5,000 times three sets of Gumbel-distributed errors ε_{n1}, ε_{n2} and ε_{n3} for a specific sample size. Using these sets of errors, the above-presented design and the assumed coefficient values, we can generate 5,000 utilities U_{n1}, U_{n2} and U_{n3}, and therefore, 5,000 hypothetical choices. Then, we can estimate 5,000 times a MNL model and draw histograms of these estimates for each parameter. This is how we can analyse, for example, the impact of the number of observations on the precision of the estimates based on the generated design.

Figure 3.2 presents histograms of 5,000 estimations of the four above-defined coefficients. The first column in Fig. 3.2 shows the histograms for 100 observations and the second row for 400 observations. This example shows, in a very simple and graphic way, two well-known findings. Firstly, the estimation of the coefficients in our MNL model by maximum likelihood is consistent, because the spread of estimations in the second column in Fig. 3.2 is narrower. Secondly, focusing on the x-axis of the histograms, the precision of the estimations of the alternative specific constants is in our case worse than the precision of the attribute coefficients. Please note that

3.3 Checking Your Statistical Design

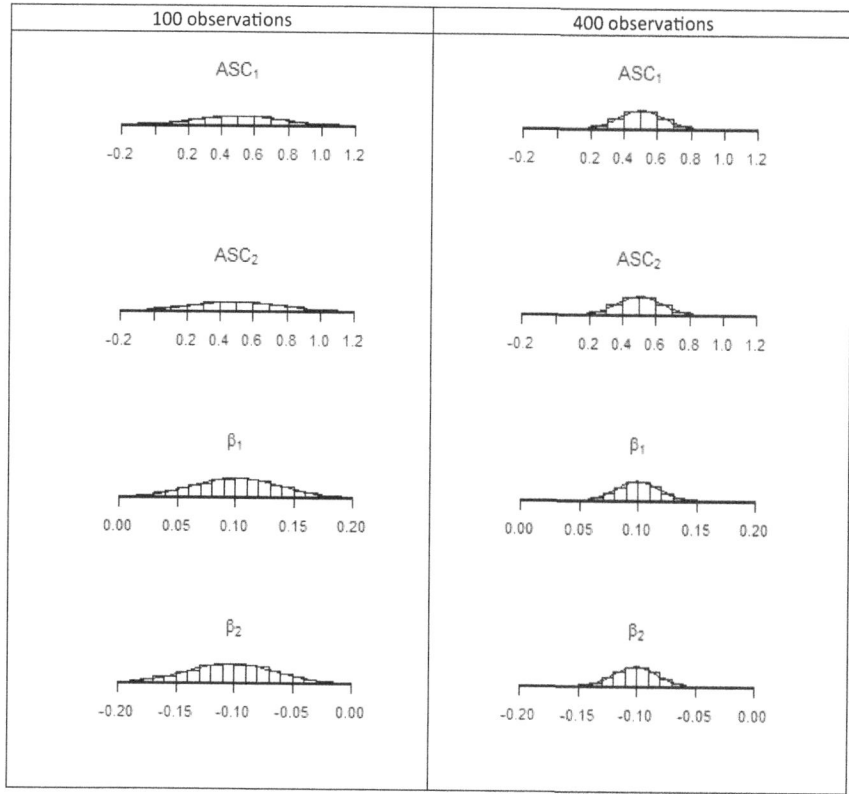

Fig. 3.2 Histograms

all histograms are centred on the assumed population value ($ASC_1 = 0.5$, $ASC_2 = 0.5$, $\beta_1 = 0.1$, $\beta_2 = -0.1$) confirming the appropriateness of the experimental design in providing unbiased estimates of the population parameter values.

References

Bliemer MCJ, Collins AT (2016) On determining priors for the generation of efficient stated choice experimental designs. J Choice Model 21:10–14. https://doi.org/10.1016/j.jocm.2016.03.001

Bliemer MCJ, Rose JM (2010) Construction of experimental designs for mixed logit models allowing for correlation across choice observations. Transp Res Part B Method 44:720–734. https://doi.org/10.1016/j.trb.2009.12.004

Bliemer MCJ, Rose JM (2011) Experimental design influences on stated choice outputs: an empirical study in air travel choice. Transp Res Part A Policy and Practice 45:63–79. https://doi.org/10.1016/j.tra.2010.09.003

Boxall P, Adamowicz WL, Moon A (2009) Complexity in choice experiments: choice of the status quo alternative and implications for welfare measurement. Aust J Agric Resource Econ 53:503–519. https://doi.org/10.1111/j.1467-8489.2009.00469.x

Boyle KJ, Özdemir S (2009) Convergent validity of attribute-based, choice questions in stated-preference studies. Environ Resource Econ 42:247–264. https://doi.org/10.1007/s10640-008-9233-9

Campbell D, Boeri M, Doherty E, George Hutchinson W (2015) Learning, fatigue and preference formation in discrete choice experiments. J Econ Behav Organ 119:345–363. https://doi.org/10.1016/j.jebo.2015.08.018

Caussade S, Ortúzar J de D, Rizzi LI, Hensher DA (2005) Assessing the influence of design dimensions on stated choice experiment estimates. Transp Res Part B Methodol 39:621–640. https://doi.org/10.1016/j.trb.2004.07.006

ChoiceMetrics (2018) Ngene 1.2 user manual & reference guide. Australia

Czajkowski M, Giergiczny M, Greene WH (2014) Learning and fatigue effects revisited: investigating the effects of accounting for unobservable preference and scale heterogeneity. Land Econ 90:324–351. https://doi.org/10.3368/le.90.2.324

Deshazo JR, Fermo G (2002) Designing choice sets for stated preference methods: the effects of complexity on choice consistency. J Environ Econ Manage 44:123–143

Greiner R, Bliemer M, Ballweg J (2014) Design considerations of a choice experiment to estimate likely participation by north Australian pastoralists in contractual biodiversity conservation. J Choice Model 10:34–45. https://doi.org/10.1016/j.jocm.2014.01.002

Hensher DA (2006) Revealing differences in willingness to pay due to the dimensionality of stated choice designs: an initial assessment. Environ Resource Econ 34:7–44. https://doi.org/10.1007/s10640-005-3782-y

Hess S, Stathopoulos A, Daly A (2012) Allowing for heterogeneous decision rules in discrete choice models: an approach and four case studies. Transportation 39:565–591. https://doi.org/10.1007/s11116-011-9365-6

Jacobsen JB, Thorsen BJ (2010) Preferences for site and environmental functions when selecting forthcoming national parks. Ecol Econ 69:1532–1544. https://doi.org/10.1016/j.ecolecon.2010.02.013

Louviere JJ, Lancsar E (2009) Choice experiments in health: the good, the bad, the ugly and toward a brighter future. Health Econ Policy Law 4:527–546. https://doi.org/10.1017/S1744133109990193

Meyerhoff J, Mariel P, Bertram C, Rehdanz K (2017) Matching preferences or changing them? The influence of the number of choice alternatives. In: 23rd Annual Conference of the European Association of Environmental and Resource Economists. Athens, Greece

Meyerhoff J, Oehlmann M, Weller P (2015) The Influence of design dimensions on stated choices in an environmental context. Environ Resource Econ 61:385–407. https://doi.org/10.1007/s10640-014-9797-5

Oehlmann M, Meyerhoff J, Mariel P, Weller P (2017) Uncovering context-induced status quo effects in choice experiments. J Environ Econ Manage 81:59–73. https://doi.org/10.1016/j.jeem.2016.09.002

Olsen SB, Meyerhoff J (2017) Will the alphabet soup of design criteria affect discrete choice experiment results? Eur Rev Agric Econ 44:309–336. https://doi.org/10.1093/erae/jbw014

Reed Johnson F, Lancsar E, Marshall D et al (2013) Constructing experimental designs for discrete-choice experiments: report of the ISPOR conjoint Analysis experimental design good research Practices task force. Value in Health 16:3–13. https://doi.org/10.1016/j.jval.2012.08.2223

Rolfe J, Bennett J (2009) The impact of offering two versus three alternatives in choice modelling experiments. Ecol Econ 68:1140–1148. https://doi.org/10.1016/j.ecolecon.2008.08.007

Sarrias M (2020) Individual-specific posterior distributions from Mixed Logit models: properties, limitations and diagnostic checks. J Choice Model 100224. https://doi.org/10.1016/j.jocm.2020.100224

References

Street DJ, Bunch DS, Moore BJ (2001) Optimal designs for 2k paired comparison experiments. Commun Stat Theory Methods 30:2149–2171. https://doi.org/10.1081/STA-100106068

Street DJ, Burgess L (2007) The construction of optimal stated choice experiments: theory and methods. Wiley, United States

Street DJ, Burgess L, Louviere JJ (2005) Quick and easy choice sets: constructing optimal and nearly optimal stated choice experiments. Int J Res Mark 22:459–470. https://doi.org/10.1016/j.ijresmar.2005.09.003

Train K (2009) Discrete choice methods with simulation, 2nd edn. Cambridge University Press, New York

van Cranenburgh S, Rose JM, Chorus CG (2018) On the robustness of efficient experimental designs towards the underlying decision rule. Transp Res Part A Policy Pract 109:50–64. https://doi.org/10.1016/j.tra.2018.01.001

Vossler CA, Doyon M, Rondeau D (2012) Truth in consequentiality: theory and field evidence on discrete choice experiments. Am Econ J Microecon 4:145–171. https://doi.org/10.1257/mic.4.4.145

Weller P, Oehlmann M, Mariel P, Meyerhoff J (2014) Stated and inferred attribute non-attendance in a design of designs approach. J Choice Model 11:43–56. https://doi.org/10.1016/j.jocm.2014.04.002

Yao RT, Scarpa R, Rose JM, Turner JA (2015) Experimental design criteria and their behavioural efficiency: an evaluation in the field. Environ Resource Econ 62:433–455. https://doi.org/10.1007/s10640-014-9823-7

Zhang J, Adamowicz WL (2011) Unraveling the choice format effect: a context-dependent random utility model. Land Economics 87:730–743. https://doi.org/10.3368/le.87.4.730

Open Access This chapter is licensed under the terms of the Creative Commons Attribution 4.0 International License (http://creativecommons.org/licenses/by/4.0/), which permits use, sharing, adaptation, distribution and reproduction in any medium or format, as long as you give appropriate credit to the original author(s) and the source, provide a link to the Creative Commons license and indicate if changes were made.

The images or other third party material in this chapter are included in the chapter's Creative Commons license, unless indicated otherwise in a credit line to the material. If material is not included in the chapter's Creative Commons license and your intended use is not permitted by statutory regulation or exceeds the permitted use, you will need to obtain permission directly from the copyright holder.

Chapter 4
Collecting the Data

Abstract This chapter discusses aspects related to data collection. It focuses, firstly, on sampling issues and, secondly, on the survey mode. Sampling issues include sample size and the type of sampling that enable precise estimates to be obtained. Regarding the survey mode, discrete choice experiments can be implemented by mail, telephone, face-to-face or web surveys. Each of these survey modes has its advantages and shortcomings. They are described and compared in the course of this chapter, addressing an important decision in the planning process of a discrete choice experiment.

4.1 Sampling Issues

Most SP studies implicitly or explicitly aim for "representative samples" and generalisable results. This implies that the survey population, the persons, households, etc., which shall be generalised has to be known (Dillman et al. 2008). It further demands an appropriate sampling frame, a list from which the sample is drawn. Two well-known errors are the coverage error (a non-sampling error), referring to units in the survey population with a non-zero probability of being included in the survey, and the sampling error which refers to only collecting data from a subset and not all units of the sampling frame. The coverage error is present if, for example, all users of an environmental good comprise the population, but researchers sample from a household register that does not include all users, i.e. the sampling frame is not complete covering the intended population of interest. An error would occur if users who are not included in the household register have characteristics that differ from those included in the register. A sampling error is present if not all members of a population are included in the sample and figures such as mean values and willingness-to-pay estimates based on this sample differ from those based on the population. To some extent, all statistics based on a sample are biased, yet the precision of the estimates varies with the type of sample and sample size. Sample weights can be used to take sampling error into account; however, they will not overcome the weaknesses of a sampling approach (such as non-probability samples, see, e.g., Yeager et al. 2011).

Given that the survey population is known, a simple random sample can be drawn if lists of households, postal addresses or e-mail addresses are available. Then a computer program can be used that numbers respondents and randomly selects them. A stratified sample, separate and disproportionate samples for specific groups, can be employed if some groups of the population have a greater chance of being included in the survey. Coverage error can be especially problematic with web surveys (Couper 2000; Bonnichsen and Olsen 2016), as for example not all individuals in a population might have access to or use the Internet, or it is difficult to construct a list with all individuals with Internet and web access, from which a random sample can be generated. There are many survey organisations (panel providers), which offer web surveys and samples for web surveys based on so-called access panels. These panel providers differ in their sampling approaches and this can make a big difference in terms of survey quality and sampling error. While some providers work with opt-in panels, where individuals volunteer to take part in surveys, others recruit panel members "offline" using, for example, a random telephone sample design (or a mix of sample designs) to reduce sampling error. Clearly, the latter approach based on some kind of probability-based sample design results in better samples and survey quality (Yeager et al. 2011). In general, generalisations for a population are strictly speaking not possible from non-probability samples. This also applies to using social media like Facebook, Twitter, etc., to recruit survey participants for web surveys. Here respondents typically select themselves for the survey, and social media users can differ from the rest of the population, which can cause biased samples. Also, large web survey samples do not automatically mean that the data are more valid and generalisable (see, e.g., Savage et al. 2013; Mills 2014 for a web survey with over 160,000 respondents and a massive sample error).

With respect to users of an environmental good, the population (e.g. users of a national park) is often not known and DCEs may be conducted onsite (e.g. in the national park), or offsite by using a mail or web survey of the citizens in a region or a country. In this case, it might be advisable to collect data over different days and times of day and to work with quota (e.g. for gender, age and education) in order to obtain some control over the sampling process and to make sure that different user groups are represented in the sample. Respondents can be determined by a systematic approach such as asking every tenth person to take part in the survey.

Often the survey population, e.g. the market size, is not known and has to be estimated (see Glenk et al. 2020 for an overview). The market size refers to the distance between the environmental good/resource and the point where WTP drops to zero (e.g. Bateman et al. 2006). In many cases, this might not correspond with political jurisdictions. In general, the definition of the market can be challenging. For example, in research on the value of national parks it is important to differentiate between users of parks and non-users, where both groups can receive benefits from the park in terms of use and/or non-use values. Therefore, it has to be decided whether all citizens in a country belong to the study population (the "market"), citizens in regions close to the park, or only citizens who actually use the park, etc. Furthermore, some parks might attract visitors from different countries and, again, this can influence the market size. In order to test for market size, researchers can sample individuals living in different distances to the environmental good/resource and then examine distance decay effects, i.e. to which extent WTP for the good decreases with distance, holding everything else constant (see Glenk et al. 2020).

A question that is often raised is the sample size that is needed in a DCE study. Here, two aspects have to be differentiated. The sample size question might firstly refer to the representativeness of the data collection, i.e. how well the sample represents the underlying population and its characteristics. This is important if DCE results shall be generalised to the population and a population's preference heterogeneity regarding characteristics such as gender, age, education, income and attitudes are of interest. Secondly, it might refer to the sample size needed to obtain statistically significant parameter estimates in the choice experiment. A practical problem might be that the sample size requirements for statistically significant parameter estimates might be different from those referring to data representativeness. For example, efficient experimental designs might suggest a low number of respondents (e.g. 300); yet, in order to analyse preferences for subgroups in the data (e.g. respondents with low or high environmental concern) larger sample sizes are needed to detect differences and to represent the population at hand.

In principle, focusing on the proportions of responses, the sample size, for example, required for representing the population in a two-alternative case with a specific certainty can be calculated (see formulas presented in Dillman et al. 2008, p. 56). In order to represent a country's population in terms of socio-demographics, a sample size of around 1,000 respondents should be sufficient and this number does not depend on the size of the country. Therefore, most cross-country surveys such as the World Value Survey include between 1,000 and 1,500 respondents per country. Similarly, the minimum sample size for estimating a proportion in a multinomial case can be determined (see Louviere et al. 2000). Some recommendations regarding the sample size requirements for stated choice experiments can also be found in Rose and Bliemer (2013) and de Bekker-Grob et al. (2015). Furthermore, it is important to stress that, once the experimental design has been generated, the sample variation for the model parameters can be analysed by simulation experiments like those presented in Sect. 3.3. Depending on the complexity of the experimental design and the type of model applied, sample sizes of 300–500 respondents might be sufficient to obtain valid estimates for stated preferences. But there are many situations and models for which this sample size may not be large enough.

In general, there is a trade-off between the number of respondents and the efficiency of the experimental design: the larger the sample size, the less important it is to have a very efficient design. For smaller sample sizes, such as 300 respondents, it is important to consider that sufficient data need to be collected to represent and analyse preference heterogeneity for subgroups in a population (e.g. regarding gender, age groups, education levels, use or non-use of the good). This can be achieved by oversampling specific groups which are of interest. Moreover, small samples do not allow for precise estimation of more complex models.

Most researchers aim for a high response rate and see this as an indicator of a "good" survey. With respect to reporting response rate, the American Association for Public Opinion Research standards (AAPOR 2016) can be recommended. However, high response rates should not be confused with non-response errors if those who do not take part in a survey differ from those who take part in the survey with respect to relevant beliefs, attitudes and socio-demographic characteristics. Surveys with high response rates might have a large non-response error and might not represent the population at hand well, and surveys with low response rates might have a low non-response error (Dillman et al. 2008). Furthermore, a high response rate is not beneficial if the questionnaire itself is problematic. Evaluating the quality of a survey can be a complex task, depending on different types of errors (sampling error, coverage error, nonresponse error and measurement error) and should not be related to a single measurement of quality.

Sampling involves many decisions and trade-offs. In any case and, if possible, a random sample of the population of interest is still the best approach to reduce sample-related errors. When working with web surveys and Internet panel providers, it is important to be aware of the type of access panel and to avoid opt-in panels. Some panel providers recruit their panel members based on probability samples, which is clearly preferable to non-probability samples. Probability-based samples are also needed if the aim of the study is to reveal generalisable findings for the population (of a region, country, etc.). While, given a very efficient experimental design, small samples (e.g. 300 respondents) might be sufficient to obtain valid SP estimates, it should be kept in mind that a larger sample might be needed to investigate preference heterogeneity regarding respondents' characteristics. On the other hand, if a sample is large (e.g. around 1,000 respondents representing the population of a country), the efficiency of the experimental design becomes less important. Finally, the estimation of the market size is a challenge in many environmental valuation studies. In this regard, it could be a good idea to sample individuals/households with different distances to the environmental good/resource and to test for distance decay effects, i.e. to what extent WTP for the good decreases with distance.

4.2 Survey Mode (Internet, Face-To-Face, Postal)

In principle, choice experiments can be implemented in any survey mode: mail surveys, telephone surveys, face-to-face surveys and web surveys. While some survey modes may have specific advantages over other modes, it has to be stressed that choosing a survey mode may also depend on the research context. For example, in development research, when collecting data in a remote area setting, face-to-face interviews might be the only option (Liebe et al. 2020). Likewise, an onsite survey is mostly conducted face-to-face or self-administered at the research site. While the research context can determine the survey mode, the survey mode can also affect the sampling approach. For example, if researchers plan to use a web survey they typically work with online access panels and not a random sample from the population, depending on the panel provider (see Sect. 4.1).

Face-to-face interviews: Computer-assisted personal interviewing (CAPI) is most often employed in face-to-face interviews: the questionnaire is in the form of a

4.2 Survey Mode (Internet, Face-To-Face, Postal)

computer program; the interviewer sees items on a screen (laptop or other mobile device), reads questions to respondents and enters the answers by pressing the corresponding keys (Loosveldt 2008). The presence of an interviewer can be an advantage for clarifying questions and surveying more complex issues, also complex DCE. However, it is important to consider that given the characteristics of a face-to-face interview, an interviewer could be a source of measurement error: Social desirability bias is an example of interviewer bias—the mere presence of an interviewer leads to a "systematic underreporting of undesirable attitudes or behaviour (e.g., drug use) and the systematic over-reporting of desirable ones (e.g., voting behaviour)" (Loosveldt 2008, p. 215). Such interviewer effects can be reduced by increasing the number of interviewers or decreasing the number of interviews for each interviewer, as well as reducing intra-interviewer correlation by providing additional interviewer training to standardise behaviour, and a follow-up of interviewers and feedback during field work.

Telephone survey: This survey mode is an interview survey (Steeh 2008) although technological innovations (answering machines, call blocking, wireless communication, Internet telephony) have changed the conditions for conducting telephone surveys over the last few decades. This has also affected response rates which have declined in most western countries. Since choice experiment tasks are often complex, telephone surveys have a disadvantage because they only contain auditory channels of communication and, hence, it is difficult to keep respondents involved, so interviews have to be shorter, questions should be relatively uncomplicated and only questions with a limited number of response categories can be employed (Steeh 2008). However, it has been demonstrated that multifactorial survey experiments such as (complex) vignette studies can also be integrated in telephone surveys (e.g. Emerson et al. 2001).

Mail survey: Mail surveys can be described as consisting of "questionnaires that are sent by postal mail to a sampled individual, who is requested to complete the questionnaire and send it back; no interviewer is present and the survey is completely self-administered" (Leeuw et al. 2008, p. 243). In comparison with face-to-face interviews, they can be implemented at low costs and respondents have less time pressure to answer the survey. Visual stimuli such as pictures and choice sets can be used and there is no interviewer bias. Furthermore, respondents have a greater degree of privacy compared with survey modes involving an interviewer. However, researchers cannot control who is answering the questionnaire and can also not control in which order respondents answer the questions. It might, for example, be a problem for a study if respondents can go through all the choice tasks provided before starting to answer them but they might check for the overall best alternative and choose the status quo or opt-out alternative on all the other tasks.

Web surveys: This is a computerised, self-administered survey mode without the presence of an interviewer. DCE and randomising questions can be easily implemented in web surveys; also paradata such as response time can be automatically collected. However, it should be considered that "[i]nternet users tend to read more quickly, are more impatient, and they scan rather than carefully read the text" (Lozar Manfreda and Vehovar 2008, p. 276). In web surveys, nonverbal aspects of the survey have to be taken into account. It should be kept in mind that respondents use different web browsers, operations systems and hardware. Web surveys can be answered on different devices and with the increasing popularity of mobile phone usage around the globe respondents use mobile devices more and more frequently to answer web surveys. Recent research shows that there are systematic differences in response behaviour depending on whether the survey was answered on a personal computer or mobile device (Couper et al. 2016). This affects for example questions with an open answer format. However, the overall differences are rather small. This is also suggested in the first studies looking at mobile device effects on the results of stated choice experiments. For example, in a choice experiment on renewable energy expansion Liebe et al. (2017) do not find significant differences in WTP values for desktop and mobile device users.

Mixed-mode surveys: Combining different survey modes is a way of taking advantage of the strengths and compensating for the weaknesses of each mode (Leeuw et al. 2008). This includes having some respondents complete a questionnaire in a different mode than other respondents. Multiple modes can also be used in different stages of the survey process, e.g. in the screening and contact stage (e.g. first telephone followed by a mail survey), main data collection stage (e.g. combination of telephone survey and follow-up mail survey), follow-up stage (e.g. first mail survey followed by a telephone or web survey). Mixed-mode approaches are often employed in surveys on sensitive topics by combining face-to-face interviews and a self-administered questionnaire. This combination is also useful for DCE because more complex choice tasks can be better integrated in a self-administered mode.

Table 4.1 presents the comparison of survey models and demonstrates that no survey mode is better than all the others. For example, mail and web surveys do not suffer from interviewer effects which could be present in environmental valuation studies if the good at hand is highly socially desirable. Here mail and web surveys have an advantage over face-to-face and telephone surveys. Also mail and web surveys are less costly than face-to-face and telephone surveys. However, face-to-face surveys in particular allow for longer interviews, more complex questionnaires including choice experiment tasks, different ways of information transmission, etc. Here they have a clear advantage over all other survey modes.

While Table 4.1 implies some trade-offs when choosing a survey mode, there are aspects of DCE which suggest that web surveys have specific advantages over the other survey modes. First, randomisation of questions, choice tasks, and alternatives and attributes within choice tasks are easy to implement in web surveys, compared to mail and face-to-face surveys as well as telephone surveys (except the latter two are computer assisted). Second, visual elements such as images and short videos, that help to describe choice attributes or choice tasks, can be conveniently included in web surveys. Third, web surveys are self-administered and, hence, interviewer effects and socially desirable response behaviour are not present or less likely than in face-to-face and telephone surveys. At least compared to mail surveys, it can also be ensured that respondents in web surveys evaluate each choice set without knowing the subsequent choice sets included in the survey (i.e. they cannot screen the whole questionnaire before answering). Fourth, compared with other survey

4.2 Survey Mode (Internet, Face-To-Face, Postal)

Table 4.1 Comparison of survey modes

Aspect	Explanation	Face-to-face	Telephone	Mail	Web
Interviewer effects	"Interviewer as source of measurement error" (Loosveldt 2008, p. 214)	−−	−	0	0
Media-related factors	"Social conventions and customs associated with media used in survey mode" (Leeuw et al. 2008, p. 116)	++	+	−	−
Information transmission	Presentation of information, channels of communication, regulation of communication flow	++	−−	−	+
Complexity allowed	Choice task complexity, for example	++	−−	+	+
Length	Interview duration	++	−	+	−−
Paradata	Response time, for example	+[a]	+	−	++
Costs	Assuming that a company is conducting the survey	−−	−	+	++

Note ++ = very positive (advantage), + = rather positive (advantage), − = rather negative (disadvantage), −− = very negative (disadvantage); 0 = effect is absent
[a] In case of computer-assisted personal interviews (CAPI)

modes, valuable paradata such as response time can be collected in web surveys. Fifth, web surveys are less costly than face-to-face and telephone surveys. On the other hand, due to time constraints it is more difficult to implement very complex questionnaires online compared to face-to-face or mail surveys. Furthermore, web surveys are often not representative for a study population (e.g. citizens of a region or country) but only for the population with Internet access. Yet, this also depends on the survey panel provider, where some providers make more effort than others to represent the population at hand as closely as possible (see Sect. 4.1). Studies comparing different survey modes in stated preferences studies on environmental valuation indicate that web surveys reveal similar results as other survey modes, especially regarding willingness-to-pay values; however, once again, the presence of survey mode effects can depend on the Internet panel provider used (Olsen 2009; Lindhjem and Navrud 2011).

Choosing the survey mode for a DCE is an important decision that has to be considered in the planning process of a study and when applying for research funding. Often the survey costs are a (or the) main driver of this decision. While computer-assisted face-to-face interviews might have advantages in terms of sample representativeness, they are more expensive than web surveys. The latter have many advantages for DCE; yet, it is important to carefully select web survey panel providers and to examine how they select their panel members (e.g. whether they are recruited by telephone and it is a managed panel, or whether it is an opt-in panel where everyone can participate and the panel provider does not have a clear overview of who is taking part, see Sect. 4.1). Lastly, as stated at the beginning of this section there might be research contexts such as in developing countries where computer-assisted face-to-face interviews are the only method that can be applied on practical grounds. A more detailed discussion of survey modes is provided for example by Dillman et al. (2008) and Leeuw et al. (2008). Menegaki et al. (2016) offer noticeable insights and guidance for web surveys in the context of DCE.

References

AAPOR (2016) Response rates—an overview. Education/Resources, American Association for Public Opinion Research. https://www.aapor.org/Education-Resources/For-Researchers/Poll-Survey-FAQ/Response-Rates-An-Overview.aspx. Accessed 8 May 2020

Bateman IJ, Day BH, Georgiou S, Lake I (2006) The aggregation of environmental benefit values: welfare measures, distance decay and total WTP. Ecol Econ 60:450–460. https://doi.org/10.1016/j.ecolecon.2006.04.003

Bonnichsen O, Olsen SB (2016) Correcting for non-response bias in contingent valuation surveys concerning environmental non-market goods: an empirical investigation using an online panel. J Environ Planning Manage 59:245–262. https://doi.org/10.1080/09640568.2015.1008626

Couper M (2000) Review: web surveys: a review of issues and approaches. Public Opin Q 64:464–494. https://doi.org/10.1086/318641

Couper MP, Antoun C, Mavletova AM (2016) Mobile web surveys: a total survey error perspective. In: Total survey Error in practice: improving quality in the era of big data. https://publications.hse.ru/en/chapters/191682818. Accessed 13 Aug 2019

de Bekker-Grob EW, Donkers B, Jonker MF, Stolk EA (2015) Sample size requirements for discrete-choice experiments in healthcare: a practical guide. Patient 8:373–384. https://doi.org/10.1007/s40271-015-0118-z

Dillman DA, Smyth JD, Christian LM (2008) Internet, mail, and mixed-mode surveys: the tailored design method, 3rd Revised. Wiley, Hoboken, NJ

Emerson MO, Yancey G, Chai KJ (2001) Does race matter in residential segregation? Exploring the preferences of White Americans. Am Sociol Rev 66:922–935. https://doi.org/10.2307/3088879

Glenk K, Johnston RJ, Meyerhoff J, Sagebiel J (2020) Spatial dimensions of stated preference valuation in environmental and resource economics: methods, trends and challenges. Environ Resource Econ 75:215–242. https://doi.org/10.1007/s10640-018-00311-w

Leeuw EDD, Hox J, Dillman D (2008) International handbook of survey methodology, 1st edn. Routledge, New York, London

Liebe U, Moumouni IM, Bigler C et al (2020) Using factorial survey experiments to measure attitudes, social norms, and fairness concerns in developing countries. Sociol Methods Res 0049124117729707. https://doi.org/10.1177/0049124117729707

Lindhjem H, Navrud S (2011) Using internet in stated preference surveys: a review and comparison of survey modes. Int Rev Environ Resource Econ 5:309–351. https://doi.org/10.1561/101.00000045

Loosveldt G (2008) Face-to-face interviews. Routledge Handbooks Online

Louviere JJ, Hensher DA, Swait JD (2000) Stated choice methods analysis and applications. Cambridge University Press, Cambridge

Lozar Manfreda C, Vehovar V (2008) Internet surveys. In: de Leeuw ED, Hox JJ, Dillman DA (eds) International handbook of survey methodology. Psychology Press, New York

References

Menegaki AN, Olsen SB, Tsagarakis KP (2016) Towards a common standard—a reporting checklist for web-based stated preference valuation surveys and a critique for mode surveys. J Choice Model 18:18–50. https://doi.org/10.1016/j.jocm.2016.04.005

Mills C (2014) The Great British Class Fiasco: a comment on Savage et al. Sociology 48:437–444. https://doi.org/10.1177/0038038513519880

Olsen SB (2009) Choosing between internet and mail survey modes for choice experiment surveys considering non-market goods. Environ Resour Econ 44:591–610. https://doi.org/10.1007/s10640-009-9303-7

Rose JM, Bliemer MCJ (2013) Sample size requirements for stated choice experiments. Transportation 40:1021–1041. https://doi.org/10.1007/s11116-013-9451-z

Savage M, Devine F, Cunningham N et al (2013) A new model of social class? Findings from the BBC's Great British Class survey experiment. Sociology 47:219–250. https://doi.org/10.1177/0038038513481128

Steeh C (2008) Telephone survey. In: de Leeuw ED, Hox JJ, Dillman DA (eds) International handbook of survey methodology. Psychology Press, New York

Yeager DS, Krosnick JA, Chang L et al (2011) Comparing the accuracy of RDD telephone surveys and internet Surveys conducted with probability and non-probability samples. Public Opin Q 75:709–747. https://doi.org/10.1093/poq/nfr020

Open Access This chapter is licensed under the terms of the Creative Commons Attribution 4.0 International License (http://creativecommons.org/licenses/by/4.0/), which permits use, sharing, adaptation, distribution and reproduction in any medium or format, as long as you give appropriate credit to the original author(s) and the source, provide a link to the Creative Commons license and indicate if changes were made.

The images or other third party material in this chapter are included in the chapter's Creative Commons license, unless indicated otherwise in a credit line to the material. If material is not included in the chapter's Creative Commons license and your intended use is not permitted by statutory regulation or exceeds the permitted use, you will need to obtain permission directly from the copyright holder.

Chapter 5
Econometric Modelling: Basics

Abstract This chapter addresses basic topics related to choice data analysis. It starts by describing the coding of attribute levels and choosing the functional form of the attributes in the utility function. Next, it focuses on econometric models with special attention devoted to the random parameter mixed logit model. In this context, the chapter compares different coefficient distributions to be used, addresses specifics of the cost attribute coefficient and it pays attention to potential correlations between random coefficients. Finally, topics related to the estimation procedure such as assuring its convergence or random draws are discussed.

5.1 Coding of Attribute Levels: Effects, Dummy or Continuous

In the choice experiment literature, the two most common ways of coding attribute levels for modelling are dummy and effects coding. Most often the choice between dummy or effects coding arises when researchers consider how qualitatively (categorically) described attributes should enter the utility function, and when researchers want to relax assumptions about linearity of continuously coded attributes (see Sect. 5.2).

Consider an attribute with L levels. The (quantitative or qualitative) levels of this attribute are transformed into $L-1$ dummy variables taking a value of one if a level is present in an alternative and equalling zero if it is not. The L-th level is omitted from analysis in order to avoid perfect collinearity. The utility of the Lth level is per definition zero, and the $L-1$ parameter estimates for the dummy variables capture the utility difference relative to the omitted baseline level. However, the utility of the status quo alternative is defined to be zero with respect to this attribute. In this case, the effect of the Lth attribute level will be perfectly correlated with the constant term for the status quo alternative. This makes it impossible to independently identify the utility effect of the status quo alternative that is unrelated to the attributes characterising the non-status quo alternatives.

Effects coding implies that the effects of attribute levels are uncorrelated with a constant term for the status quo alternative. Again, $L-1$ variables are created, which receive a value of minus one if the Lth attribute level is present, and a value of one for each of the $L - 1$ attribute levels. Importantly, the utility of the reference level is directly related to utility of the $L - 1$ attribute levels, defined as the negative sum of the $L - 1$ parameter estimates. Therefore, the estimates are likely uncorrelated with the constant for the status quo alternative. See Table 1 in Daly et al. (2016, p. 38) for an example of dummy and effects coding for a 4-level attribute.

The above differences, described by Bech and Gyrd-Hansen (2005), have quickly led to the widespread belief that effects coding would be "superior" to dummy coding and that dummy coding would imply confounding between base (reference) levels of dummy-coded attributes and dummy-coded alternative-specific constants (ASCs; typically associated with either the status quo or the non-status quo alternatives).

But does it really matter if effects coding or dummy coding is used? To start with, the concern about confounding of base (reference) levels of dummy-coded attributes and ASCs is only relevant for cases where the experimental design includes an opt-out or status quo alternative, and if any of the attributes relate exclusively to non-status quo alternatives. What characterises these cases is that none of the attribute levels of the experimental design will be shared with the status quo alternative. An example may be an attribute describing spatial location (e.g. an attribute describing where proposed changes would take place) in a WTP context. If there is no policy change in the status quo option, this attribute does actually not characterise the status quo. In supply contexts (e.g. studies aimed at estimating ecosystem service suppliers' WTA to participate in contract schemes), attributes of conservation contracts (e.g. collaborative participation; contract length) do not apply for the status quo or opt-out alternative, which typically is a "no contract" alternative.

Furthermore, the estimation process of marginal values differs slightly. In a WTP context, effects coding requires taking the negative ratio of twice the utility parameter of interest, β_1, plus the sum of the utility of utility parameters associated with remaining $L - 1$ levels and the cost parameter. For example, for a 2-level effects coded attribute, marginal $WTP = -2\beta_1/\beta$ and for 3-level effects coded attribute, marginal $WTP = -(2\beta_1 + \beta_2)/\beta$. Importantly, however, whether effects coding or dummy coding is used will not affect the log-likelihood value of multinomial logit models (i.e. the models are statistically equivalent), marginal WTP or WTA estimates, nor will it affect welfare estimates of CS (using the approach proposed by Hanemann 1984). This is the most important insight and is due to the fact that what matters are differences in utility between the individual levels of an attribute (or differences in utility between alternatives). Effects coding only uses a different normalisation of the reference level, while the difference in utility between levels remains the same for either form of coding.

Apart from requiring more attention when coding and estimating WTP, effects coding can further complicate the interpretation of utility effects. Daly et al. (2016) provide an example related to imposing an equality constraint on some of the attribute levels. Overall, therefore, the reasons above seem to be sufficient to discourage the use of effects coding as a "superior" model specification. We strongly recommend that researchers consult Daly et al. (2016) for a more detailed theoretical and empirical investigation of the impacts of coding before making any decisions on whether to use effects and dummy coding. Beyond the arguments raised above, we also wish to note that the equivalence between dummy coding and effects coding disappears when random coefficients are applied to these variables (Burton 2018).

Given the above, in most cirumstances effects coding offers no additional benefits over dummy coding and may lead to some undesirable complications. However, there may be a single reason for considering effects coding, which is traced back to an argument presented by Bech and Gyrd-Hansen (2005). This relates to the aim of giving the ASC parameter (associated with a status quo) a direct (behavioural) interpretation. If, for example, the aim is to interpret the ASC parameter as evidence for status quo bias, it may be tested if the coding of attributes has a strong impact on the ASC parameter estimate. However, in DCE applications that include a monetary attribute which enters the indirect utility function in a continuous fashion, the utility difference between zero (used only for status quo) and the lowest level of the monetary attribute in the non-status quo alternatives will still be captured by the ASC (see Appendix in Hess and Beharry-Borg 2012). Hence, in most applications the constant will in any case be confounded with attributes, even if effects coding has been applied, because the cost attribute is unlikely to be effects coded to enable estimation of WTP and WTA.

In summary, for multinomial choice models (DCE data) and the most typical applications, we recommend to use dummy coding; effects coding offers no advantages while making interpretation more difficult.

5.2 Functional Form of the Attributes in the Utility Function

Following random utility theory, the utility an individual derives from choosing an alternative comprises of a deterministic, observable component and a random, unobservable component (Sect. 1.2). The most common specification of the deterministic component is linear and additive in attributes. One of the first choice experiment applications in environmental economics that introduces non-linear terms into the utility specification is Adamowicz et al. (1998). They used quadratic terms for some of the continuously coded attributes, which helped identify threshold effects for these attributes: utility increases at a diminishing rate up to a threshold, beyond which utility decreases at an increasing rate. They find that the non-linear specification outperforms the linear one. This suggests that it can be important to test and assess if indeed there is non-linearity in sensitivity towards attributes.

Perhaps the simplest and most effective way of testing for non-linearity is to use dummy coding for $L - 1$ attribute levels. The resulting estimates for each level can be directly inspected or displayed graphically to investigate if utility changes linearly to (proportionally with) changes in the attribute. Figure 5.1 presents example of two different effects the attributes can have on the utility. The effect of the first attribute (Attr. 1) is approximately linear over attribute levels and the effect of the second

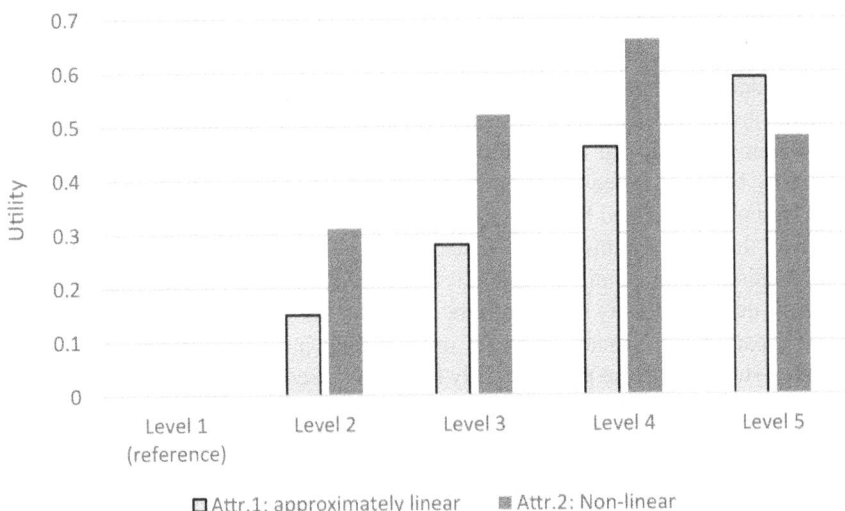

Fig. 5.1 Example of plotting utility of dummy-coded attribute levels of two 5-level attributes

attribute (Attr 2.) is non-linear. Generally, likelihood-ratio tests can be used to test if a non-linear specification outperforms a linear one. To test if utility increases proportionally over two dummy-coded attribute levels, a Wald test may be used to test if $\beta_1 - \beta_2 \left(\frac{X_2}{X_1} \right) = 0$, where X_1 and X_2 refer to quantities associated with two attribute levels and β_1 and β_2 are correspondings parameters. When investigating or plotting utility parameters of dummy or effects coded levels, care should be taken if the attribute levels are not evenly spaced so that utility differences between attribute levels relate to varying differences in quantities. If there is an indication of a non-linear utility surface across the range of attribute levels, the dummy specification can be retained, or a number of alternative options can be considered for introducing non-linearity in an attribute's utility surface.

The first is a non-linear transformation of the independent variables (attributes and/or socio-demographic variables if included). For example, this may be done through the use of polynomials (quadratic, cubic, etc.) as described above, or a logarithmic transformation. Note that the resulting specification is still linear and additive in parameters—merely the utility of an attribute will be described by a non-linear function. Non-linear transformation may also include Box-Cox, Box-Tukey, or alternative power transformations. Examples of the use of such applications include Farsi (2010), Glenk and Colombo (2013) and Tuhkanen et. al. (2016) (see also Stathopoulos and Hess 2011 for a transportation application). Non-linear transformation does not make sense for 2-level attributes, and the advantages of a non-linear transformation over simple dummy coding may be questioned for 3-level attributes. As an aside, of course any of the above non-linear transformations may also be applied to socio-demographic variables included in the model (as interactions with attributes,

5.2 Functional Form of the Attributes in the Utility Function

as independent variables explaining class membership in latent class models or as part of structural equations in hybrid choice models).

A second approach is the use of a piecewise specification (splines). Assume a continuous attribute with five attribute levels ranging from 10 to 100 (10, 30, 60, 80, 100). The "dummy specification test" described above suggests marginal utility is not significantly different between 10 and 30, then increases but is not different between 30 and 60, then increases again but is constant between 60 and 100. In this case, the following three categories and corresponding dummy variables could be created (as opposed to five dummy variables, of which four enter the utility function for the "dummy specification test"): X_1: [10–30[= 1, otherwise 0; X_2: [30–60[= 1, otherwise 0; [60–100] = 1, otherwise 0. With one acting as a reference category, two of the above dummies can be entered into the utility function. This will produce two utility parameters corresponding to the attribute-level intervals defined above. However, this approach has the drawback that marginal utility is zero within the intervals, and the resulting function is discontinuous (there are discrete steps or "jumps", see Fig. 5.2). One alternative is to use a piecewise linear specification. Marginal utility is allowed to vary within intervals and a continuous function is enforced (i.e. no "jumps", see Fig. 5.2)—in the example above this may be relevant if marginal utility is found not to be zero within intervals but is, for example, increasing, but at different rates. For the example above, three variables are specified as follows: $X_1 = \min(x, 30)$; $X_2 = \max(0, \min(x - 30, 30))$; $X_3 = \max(0, \min(x - 60, 40))$, where x describes the value of the initial attribute level. A piecewise linear specification can be useful in choice experiment applications that investigate some form of

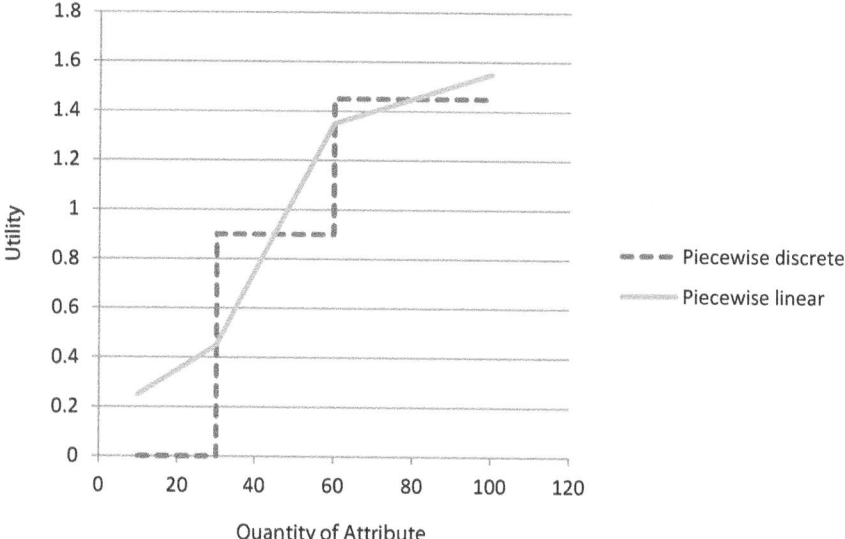

Fig. 5.2 Example of piecewise discrete and piecewise linear functional forms

reference dependency (Lanz et al. 2010; Ahtiainen et al. 2015). Combining the polynomial approach with the piecewise approach can result in a piecewise non-linear specification (Glenk 2011).

The use of any type of non-linear specification for the utility of attributes implies that marginal WTP/WTA estimates depend on the attribute value, i.e. there is no unique estimate, but values differ for different levels of provision of an attribute. Sensitivity to cardinally scaled attributes (e.g., distance in km, area in km^2, frequency, percentage change, change in objects that can be counted) may not change at a constant rate. Such non-linear utility effects can sometimes be motivated by economic theory, for example, through the principle of diminishing marginal utility. See Sagebiel et al. (2017) for an example related to changes in forest cover, or Glenk et al. (2011) for an example related to water quality improvements.

It can be easily assessed if non-linearity in the utility surface is present by using dummy coding of attribute levels. If there is an indication of a non-linearity, the dummy specification can be retained, or a number of alternative options for specifying the observed part of utility for an attribute can be considered. Such non-linear transformations might be more convenient compared to a dummy specification if the attribute entails at least three, but is better if there are more than three levels. When reporting marginal WTP/WTA estimates for attributes based on non-linear specifications, researchers should clarify the corresponding level of provision that underpins the estimate. With reference to Sect. 1.1, one should be reluctant to introduce any form of non-linearity on the cost coefficient to maintain valid welfare estimates.

Finally, a practical challenge with the testing of different functional forms of attributes, relates to the design and how the attribute was specified there (see Chap. 3). If, for example, a D-efficient design is generated assuming a continuous attribute, and we want to code it using dummy levels, the results obtained may not reflect the underlying preferences. Thus, care should be taken when the functional form deviates from the design (see Sect. 3.3).

5.3 Econometric Models

5.3.1 Multinomial (Conditional) Logit

The econometrics literature makes a distinction between the multinomial logit and the conditional logit model. In practice, the two labels are often used interchangeably. The term multinomial refers to a situation where more than two alternatives are available to consumers (or respondents). Both the multinomial and the conditional logit model aim at explaining the observed choices. The distinction between the multinomial and the conditional model arises in the use of explanatory variables.

The multinomial logit model explains the observed choices only by means of characteristics of the individuals (e.g. gender and age). The conditional logit model, as introduced by McFadden (1974), allows choices to be explained by means of variables describing the characteristics of the available alternatives (e.g. quality and cost). The latter are henceforth denoted as (product) attributes. It is good practice to use a combination of individual and attribute specific variables in discrete choice models. As a result, a more general model combining the multinomial and conditional logit formulations is commonly used, hence explaining the inconsistent use of terminology. To avoid confusion, this document will refer to the above general model as the MNL model. Moreover, the two models are identical from a mathematical perspective (see also Greene 2017; Long 1997).

Chapter 2 in Train (2009) makes the connection between the MNL model both as a behavioural and as an econometric model. It should be noted that the econometric flexibility offered by the MNL model (and more advanced choice models) is not always in line with the behavioural restrictions imposed by, for example, economic theory (e.g. Batley and Ibañez-Rivas 2013). Section 2.5 in Train (2009) is particularly important as it highlights a number of identification issues related to the MNL model with significant implications for the use of constants, sociodemographic variables and scale parameters in the MNL model.

5.3.2 *Mixed Logit Models—Random Parameter, Error Component and Latent Class Models*

Mixed logit models (MXL), including the random parameters MXL (RP-MXL), error components MXL (EC-MXL) and latent class models (LCM), extend the MNL model by allowing for unobserved heterogeneity in the estimated parameters. While in the MNL model, the estimated preference parameters are fixed, MXL models allow preferences to vary across choices (Brownstone and Train 1998—also known as cross-sectional modelling), individuals (Revelt and Train 1998—also known as panel modelling) or both (Hess and Rose 2009—also known as inter-and-intra respondent heterogeneity).

The MXL assumes the unobserved heterogeneity follows a continuous or discrete distribution across the population. In the early years of its application, the discrete distributions were represented by LCM and the continuous distributions were restricted usually to univariate normal densities.

However, the unrestricted domain (negative and positive values between minus and plus infinity) of the normal density goes against many behavioural predictions, such as negative cost sensitivities. We often know whether an attribute has a positive or negative influence on utility and this has resulted in the implementation of alternative distributional forms, such as the log-normal density (e.g. Train and Sonnier 2005). Also, correlations between preferences across distributions have been implemented to make the models more flexible (see again Train and Sonnier 2005). Another important extension has been the introduction of willingness-to-pay space models, as will be shown in Sect. 6.1 (Train and Weeks 2005; Daly et al. 2012a).

The extensions of the MNL and MXL, particularly beyond univariate normal densities and working in willingness-to-pay space, have significant implications on the data and estimation requirements. First, a significant number of draws need to be taken to accurately approximate the integral in the likelihood function (Train 2009, Chap. 6) and alternative routines (e.g. Halton, MLHS and Sobol) to draw from the specified densities might work better than others (Bhat 2003; Hess et al. 2006; Czajkowski and Budziński 2019). Irrespective of the number of draws, the standard classical maximum simulated likelihood method struggles with the complexity of the MXL, especially when multivariate distributions are included in the model specification. Moreover, robustness across starting values and the number of draws needs to be tested, but alternative estimation strategies, such as Bayesian analysis (Huber and Train 2001), Expectation Maximisation (see Train 2009, Chap. 14) or Maximum Approximate Composite Marginal Likelihood (Bhat and Sidharthan 2011) have been proposed.

A special case of the MXL is the EC-MXL (Scarpa et al. 2005). The error component acts as an additional error term in the utility function and is either implemented at the cross-sectional or panel level. Most applications now adopt a panel specification, that is more than one choice occasion per respondent. The benefit of the additional error term is that it allows for different correlation patterns across alternatives and thereby alleviates the Independence of Irrelevant Alternatives assumption underlying the MNL model. A common application is that of an additional error component on the status quo and none on the hypothetical alternatives in the choice set. The error component is modelled as a zero mean continuously (normally) distributed variable such that only the variance term needs to be estimated. That can easily lead to identification issues as can be the case of error components and random alternative specific constants. Important identification and normalisation strategies are discussed in Walker et al. (2007).

Discrete mixed logit (DM-MXL) and LCMs move away from the continuously distributed random parameters specification. Instead, they assume the random parameter(s) can only take a limited (discrete) number of values and each mass point is associated with a probability (Hess 2014). Hence, for each discrete random parameter K location and $(K-1)$ probabilities need to be estimated. Here, K refers to the number of mass points and since the probabilities need to sum to one, one probability parameter cannot be estimated. In estimation, the number of combinations between mass points and the total number of parameters rapidly increases with the number of random parameters included. For this reason, the DM-MXL model is hardly applied in practice. Instead, the LCM has gained much more in popularity (Greene and Hensher 2003). Like the DM-MXL model, the LCM assumes a finite number of potential values for the random parameters, but assumes there exists correlation across some of the random parameters in the model—preference parameters are random (discrete), but assumed the same for several "classes" of preferences. In addition, a probability of each respondents' membership in each class is estimated (and can be made a function of their socio-demographic characteristics). As a result, there is a probability of belonging to a class. More recent versions of the LCM allow for random parameter heterogeneity within classes (e.g. Greene and Hensher 2013; Campbell et al. 2014; Karlõševa et al. 2016).

The LCM has often been misinterpreted due to its behavioural appeal. Many applications forget that class membership is only known up to a probability and each respondent has a finite probability of belonging to each class. Mean probability of belonging to each class is not the same as a share of respondents belonging to each class. Moreover, LCMs are even more subject to local maxima and convergence issues than the conventional MXL. The EM-algorithm is very effective in estimating LCMs, but even then, robustness checks using a wide range of starting values are of the utmost importance. Recent improvements in the estimation of LCMs with a large number of mass points and flexible mixing densities are reported in Train (2016).

5.3.3 G-MXL Model

The generalised mixed logit (G-MXL) model (Fiebig et al. 2010; Greene and Hensher 2010) received significant attention for its acclaimed ability to separate preference and scale heterogeneity. As argued by Hess and Rose (2012), this claim is incorrect, because preferences and scale are confounded and the interpretation of the estimated parameters as preferences or scale is always the arbitrary decision of the researcher. Some forms of the G-MXL model can be seen as a middle-ground between the RP-MXL model without correlated parameters and the RP-MXL model with fully correlated parameters, as G-MXL introduces a single additional parameter capturing simultaneous correlation between all parameters, rather than modelling all correlations separately, which requires many more parameters. Overall, the model is now rarely used, because of the problems with the interpretation of the estimated correlation coefficient, which cannot be definitely attributed to scale heterogeneity. However, its specific versions can still be useful, provided they are correctly interpreted (e.g. Keane and Wasi 2013; Hess and Train 2017).

5.3.4 Hybrid Choice Models

Besides the use of socio-economic characteristics (such as age and gender), it is often useful to explain the observed choices by means of attitudes or other not directly observable constructs (latent behavioural traits). For example, assume one wishes to explain the decision to buy an electric car by the extent to which the respondent is "environmentally friendly". Attitudinal statements included in surveys measure the degree of environmental friendliness of respondents. However, these responses are associated with measurement error and introducing them directly in the choice model may result in endogeneity issues. Therefore, we instead try to explain the observed choices (the choice model) and responses to attitudinal statements (the measurement model) by means of the same underlying latent variable. In addition, the structural component can be added, which explains how latent environmental friendliness varies across respondents with respect to their socio-demographic characteristics. While the hybrid choice model (HCM, sometimes called integrated choice and latent variable—ICLV model) addresses the measurement error of indicator variables, to date there has only been limited attention to the extent that the HCM addresses endogeneity as opposed to more traditional instrumental variable approaches or alternatives (Hoyos et al. 2015; Budziński and Czajkowski 2018; Mariel et al. 2018; Guevara et al. 2018).

Hybrid choice models can be estimated simultaneously or sequentially. The former is more efficient, but makes the estimation more complex and slower due to the use of additional integrals in the likelihood function. Estimation times can be significantly reduced by means of Bayesian estimation (e.g. Dekker et al. 2016). Mariel and Meyerhoff (2016) show that the use of hybrid models is justified when one is primarily interested in learning about preference heterogeneity, but not in predictive power.

Chorus and Kroessen (2014) represent the main source of criticism of the HCM when commenting on its use in transportation. Their first point of criticism is that HCMs do not support the derivation of travel demand policies that aim to change travel behaviour through changes in a latent variable, because of the non-trivial endogeneity of the latent variable regarding travel choice. Their second point is that the cross-sectional nature of the latent variable does not allow for claims concerning changes in the variable at the individual level.

Vij and Walker (2016) present a comprehensive comparison between MXL and HCM concluding that HCM can lead to an improvement in the analyst's ability to predict outcomes in the choice data, and it allows for the identification of structural relationships between variables that could not otherwise be identified by a choice model without latent variables. Moreover, HCM can help correct for bias arising from omitted variables and measurement error, it can in some cases reduce the variance of the parameter estimates, and, finally, it can quantify the impact of latent constructs on observable behaviour, preferences and WTP and demand elasticities (e.g. Boyce et al. 2019; Czajkowski et al. 2017a, b; Zawojska et al. 2019).

The latest discussion in the HCM literature points to perceptions and their use in HCM. For example, Bahamonde-Birke et al. (2017) discuss the differences between attitudes and perceptions and Borriello and Rose (2019) highlight the difference between global and localised attitudinal responses. The potential of perceptions within HCMs has thus far been largely overlooked in environmental valuation.

5.4 Coefficient Distribution in RP-MXL

Choosing the correct distribution to capture the heterogeneity in underlying population preferences has been one of the major research interests in DCE in recent years, but it is still a central problem. Extensive literature exists on this subject (Daly et al. 2012b; Dekker 2016; Fosgerau and Bierlaire 2007; Fosgerau and Mabit 2013; Scarpa

5.4 Coefficient Distribution in RP-MXL

et al. 2008a; Train 2016), but the question of choosing the correct distribution still seems to be open.

Before we analyse the type of distribution to be used for our coefficients, we could test whether they should be considered random. The z-statistics of the estimated deviations of the random parameters are usually used to test this. An alternative and more sophisticated way to test the randomness of a coefficient is the Lagrange Multiplier (LM) test proposed by McFadden and Train (2000). Mariel et al. (2013), however, show that, on the one hand, the z-statistic test usually has high power achieved at the expense of a distorted empirical size and that, on the other hand, the LM test has very low power.

A model in which all parameters are assumed to be random is more flexible than a model in which some of the parameters are assumed to be non-random. Obviously, this flexibility is achieved at the expense of the loss of degrees of freedom. Nevertheless, it is better to work with a more flexible model by assuming that all parameters are random than imposing incorrect constraints on the randomness of the parameters.

If a parameter is assumed to be random, the distributions of monetary and non-monetary attributes are often set to normal. But that distribution choice can cause serious problems in the WTP calculation. The distribution of WTP for an attribute is generally derived from the distribution of the ratio of coefficients corresponding to the non-monetary and monetary attribute. Since the monetary coefficient enters the denominator, its distribution is crucial for the distribution of WTP. Daly et al. (2012b) show that some popular distributions used for the monetary coefficient in random coefficient models, including normal, truncated normal, uniform and triangular, can imply infinite moments for the distribution of WTP, even if truncated or bounded at zero. Therefore, their mechanical application to the monetary coefficient may lead to undefined moments of the distribution (e.g. mean). To avoid that problem, the analyst can interpret quantiles of the distribution (e.g. median), adopt other distributions for the monetary coefficient (e.g. log-normal) or re-parameterise the model in WTP space (Sect. 6.1). It is important to note that if a log-normal distribution is assumed, then the interpretation of the estimated parameters (β) and standard deviation (σ) is not straightforward, as the median, mean and standard deviation of the distribution are given by $\exp(\beta)$, $\exp(\beta + \sigma^2/2)$ and $\exp(\beta + \sigma^2/2) \cdot \sqrt{\exp(\sigma^2) - 1}$ respectively.

Independently of the type of distribution used, a wide spread of the preferences often means extreme preferences for a non-marginal share of respondents and in this case, a pre-analysis of the data is needed. It can indicate lexicographic, non-trading or protest responses that can require a specific treatment (Hess et al. 2010).

The analyst can also properly test the coefficients' distribution by the use of the Fosgerau and Bierlaire (2007) semi-nonparametric test for mixing distributions in discrete choice models. It tests if a random parameter follows an a priori postulated distribution. Unfortunately, it is not included in standard software packages with the exception of Biogeme (Bierlaire 2020). A less sophisticated but simpler procedure is proposed by Hensher and Greene (2003). They suggest plotting the contributions (incremental marginal utility) of all individuals to the overall sample mean parameter estimate and hence the profile of individual preference heterogeneity. It is a procedure which is easy to perform with any software package and although it is not a proper statistical test, it can give an idea of the underlying distributions of the parameters. Alternatively, Fosgerau and Mabit (2013) propose a method to generate flexible mixture distributions. Their proposal takes draws from a distribution and transforms them using a power series. It allows for a use of a flexible and non-standard distribution without restrictive assumptions. In general, there is still limited information for practitioners regarding the performance of the above-described tests and approaches.

If the underlying theory implies a specific sign of the coefficient (e.g. negative sign for cost coefficient) a log-normal (with changed or unchanged sign) can be used. In other cases, the normal distribution can be appropriate bearing in mind that wide standard deviations indicate inappropriateness of the assumed distribution. If the focus of the analysis is on WTP, the model can be estimated in WTP space (Sect. 6.1). If there is a clear indication that the distribution of the parameters is non-standard (non-symmetric, bi-modal) some of the flexible, but technically complex, parametric (e.g. LCM) or non-parametric approaches can be applied (Train 2016).

5.5 Specifics for the Cost Attribute

The cost coefficient is one of the most important elements of the choice model. Indeed, when one treats a choice model as an econometric model, the cost coefficient is just like any other explanatory variable in the model. Similarly, when the choice model is a (non-economic) behavioural model, then prices and their corresponding coefficients simply describe how the attractiveness of an alternative varies as a function of its price. However, we often treat the choice model as an economic model and wish to use it to obtain welfare measures expressed in terms of WTP or WTA. By working in a RUM context, we implicitly assume the respondent maximises his/her utility subject to a budget constraint (Small and Rosen 1981). For the indirect utility function, which we estimate and specify in the choice model, to be consistent with economic theory the utility function needs to be linear in price when conditional demand is restricted to unity (Batley and Ibáñez Rivas 2013). If that is not the case, any estimated welfare measure is invalid. When the utility function is linear for prices, then the negative of the cost coefficient measures the marginal utility of income and can be used to translate utilities into monetary terms. In effect, this is what the WTP-space model (see Sect. 6.1) does directly (Train and Weeks 2005). For this reason, we also often use a negative log-normal density to describe any preference heterogeneity in the cost coefficient (Daly et al. 2012b).

While for simplicity of the calculation of WTP some applications assume the monetary attribute parameter to be fixed, this is discouraged, as heterogeneity with respect to the monetary variable is almost always substantial, and constraining it introduces significant bias to the model and the estimated WTP. This point is analysed further in Sect. 6.1.

5.6 Correlation Between Random Coefficients

McFadden and Train (2000) showed that any choice model, with any distribution of preferences, can be approximated to any degree of accuracy by a mixed logit, demonstrating that this is a highly flexible model. Nevertheless, Train and Weeks (2005) show that widely applied models with uncorrelated utility coefficients imply that scale is constant across all utilities and implies that corresponding WTP values are correlated in a very particular way. Similarly, a model specified in WTP space with uncorrelated parameters implies a specific pattern of correlation in utility coefficients (Carson and Czajkowski 2019).

The assumed distributions of random coefficients and their possible correlations impose specific restrictions, which should be in line with the actual respondents' behaviour. Correlations among utility coefficients can arise for many reasons and have been observed in different fields (Revelt and Train 1998; Scarpa et al. 2008b; Hess and Train 2017). The most general form of a RP-MXL allows all utility coefficients to be randomly distributed and correlated. It allows for the type of correlation that would result from behavioural sources as well as scale heterogeneity. It is not possible to empirically determine what portion is due to behavioural sources and what portion of an estimated correlation is due to scale heterogeneity. In the case of behavioural source, people who support one attribute can also be supportive of the second attribute, creating a positive correlation between the coefficients of the two attributes (Mariel and Meyerhoff 2018).

In the case of scale heterogeneity, the correlation appears to be due to the fact that a respondent's choice can be more random (with all of the coefficients being smaller) or more deterministic (with all of the coefficients being larger in magnitude). The scale of utility, that is the magnitude of all utility coefficients, differs across individuals. According to Hess and Train (2017), it is impossible to empirically distinguish various sources of heterogeneity. A RP-MXL with full covariance among coefficients includes not only correlation induced by scale heterogeneity but also any other source of correlation. They recommend estimating a RP-MXL with full covariance if the aim is to allow for all forms of correlation among utility coefficients. The estimation of such a model is more complex than estimating a model with uncorrelated coefficients, given the high number of parameters and possible non-concave areas of the log-likelihood function, but software packages which do this are widely available.

In summary, if enough data is available to warrant identification and convergence of the model, allowing for correlations of random parameters is highly recommended. This is especially important for utility functions with dummy-coded attribute levels and error component models.

5.7 Assuring Convergence

There are many papers in the literature presenting estimations of different discrete choice models without giving any details regarding the estimation procedure. This estimation procedure is usually a maximum likelihood estimator or a maximum simulated likelihood estimator. If we focus on the most applied models, the maximised likelihood function is globally concave only for a multinomial logit model, whereas the likelihood function or simulated likelihood function of MXL models or HCMs is, generally, not globally concave and may feature several local maxima. The selection of starting values is a crucial issue to avoid an inferior local maximum. Empirical studies rarely describe the choice of starting values used and there are not many studies devoted to this topic, and, unfortunately, little guidance to solve this issue exists.

The work of Hole and Yoo (2017) is an exception in this regard, as it proposes an estimation strategy based on the joint use of heuristic optimisation algorithms and the usual gradient-based algorithms to obtain the estimates from different models through a simulated maximum likelihood method. The central idea is to use heuristic algorithms to locate a starting point which is likely to be close to the global maximum, and then to use gradient-based algorithms to refine this point further. Their results based on simulation studies indicate that repeatedly finding a particular maximum from several starting points is not reliable proof that this is in fact the global maximum and their strategy generally results in higher maxima than more conventional estimation strategies.

Optimisation procedures like Newton–Raphson, BHHH, BFGS or Nelder-Mead, usually implemented in software packages, can end up easily in local maxima in relatively simple MXL models. It is important to bear in mind that convergence to the global maximum of the likelihood function or simulated likelihood function is not guaranteed by any of these optimisation algorithms. Their performance is case specific and it is difficult to give a general recommendation. Nevertheless, it is strongly recommended to always estimate more complex models a couple of times with different starting values, different optimisation procedures and, if possible, use a mixture of heuristic procedures and the usual gradient-based algorithms as indicated by Hole and Yoo (2017).

Mebane and Sekhon (2011) is another example of a similar approach that combines evolutionary search algorithms with derivative-based (Newton or quasi-Newton) methods to solve difficult optimisation problems. Their procedure finds a global maximum of functions that are not globally concave and they may even have irregularities such as saddle points or discontinuities. The generally implemented optimisation methods such as Newton–Raphson, BHHH, BFGS or Nelder-Mead that rely on derivatives of the objective function may be in these cases unable to find any optimum at all. The only drawback of heuristic search methods is that the computation time is usually much higher than that necessary for gradient-based optimisation.

5.7 Assuring Convergence

As a general recommendation, the researcher can always use different sets of random starting values and compare the final value of the log-likelihood function. On the other hand, MNL estimates should be reasonable starting values for an RP-MXL model without correlations, and RP-MXL estimates without correlations should provide reasonable starting values for RP-MXL with correlations. If it is a RP-MXL model with normally distributed coefficients, the means can be set to the MNL estimates, standard deviation to a small positive constant (e.g. 0.5) and the remaining coefficients related to the covariances of the random coefficient can be set to zero. It is important to highlight that very often the LCM ends up in flat regions of its log-likelihood function. The more dummy variables are included in a model, the more the severe problem of a flat region is likely to appear. If we do not have any a priori hypothesis about the coefficients in different classes of our LCM that could function as starting values in each class, the model should be estimated repeatedly for randomly generated starting values.

There are other ways to reduce the problems with the optimisation procedures. The magnitude of a coefficient multiplying an explanatory variable (usually an attribute) in a discrete choice model is related to the scale of this variable. If the scale of the variable is thousands of units, the corresponding coefficient is expected to be in order of thousandths. The higher the differences in orders of the coefficients, the more difficult it will be for the optimiser to reach a global maximum. It is, therefore, a good practice to re-scale the attribute so that the order of all coefficients is similar (ideally between 0.1 and 1). This simple procedure will ease the convergence of the estimation procedure based on numerical optimisation. In order to recover the original units, the estimated coefficients should be multiplied or divided accordingly. For example, the values of an attribute x_1 are between 10 and 100, and its contribution to the utility is $\Phi_{1njt} = \beta_1 \cdot x_{1njt}$. If the values of this attribute are divided by 100 ($x^*_{1njt} = x_{1njt}/100$) and, therefore, values between 0.1 and 1.0 are used in the estimation process, the contribution to the utility remains the same: $\Phi_{1njt} = \beta_1 \cdot x_{1njt} = (\beta_1 \cdot 100) \cdot (x_{1njt}/100) = \beta_1^* \cdot x^*_{1njt}$. The corresponding estimated parameter $\hat{\beta}_1^* = \widehat{(\beta_1 \cdot 100)}$ should then be divided by 100 to obtain the estimation of the original β_1.

McCullough and Vinod (2003) present a four-step process for the verification of the solution obtained. The procedure is based on the detailed analysis of the final gradient and trace, hessian and quadratic approximation of the likelihood function in the proximity of the obtained solution. Practitioners should always be cautious about solutions obtained from statistical packages, no matter how convenient and expected the outcomes are, and apply at least some of the checks described above.

5.8 Random Draws in RP-MXL

Simulated maximum likelihood is the preferred estimator of most researchers dealing with discrete choice models, as it is relatively straightforward and readily implemented in most statistical software packages. Simulating the value of the log-likelihood function is necessarily associated with the simulation error that depends on the number and type of draws used. By using a different set of draws or even changing the order of explanatory variables a researcher will arrive at somewhat different estimation results, in terms of the value of the log-likelihood function, parameter estimates and their estimated standard errors (and hence the associated z-statistics).

Several studies have demonstrated the advantages of using Quasi Monte Carlo (QMC) methods in terms of reducing simulation-driven variation of the results (e.g. using Halton draws, Modified Latin Hypercube Sampling or Sobol draws rather than pseudo-random draws) and this has led to their wide proliferation. Unfortunately, examples of 100 Halton draws leading to a smaller bias than 1,000 pseudo-random draws (e.g. Bhat 2001) have in fact led some to use very few draws for simulations, when in fact not much is known about the extent of the possible bias resulting from using different numbers of different types of draws in various conditions (datasets).

One problem with using the popular Halton sequence is its poor performance in higher dimensions (i.e. generating Halton sequences for a high number of coefficients), because the sequences generated using high prime numbers as bases tend to be highly correlated. To address this problem, the use of scrambling or shuffling the sequence (or other QMC methods) has been suggested. Wang and Kockelman (2006) compared scrambled and shuffled Halton sequences, concluding that although scrambling seems to perform better, the difference is relatively small.

Using more draws is always better than using fewer—not only will the estimates become more precise (lower simulation error) but this can also lead to the detection of identification problems (Chiou and Walker 2007). Using very few draws (e.g. below 100) can therefore hinder estimation of even preliminary models, which are used by researchers to guide their subsequent analyses, i.e. the choice of the final preferred and published model. It is important to keep in mind that the estimation by maximisation of a simulated likelihood function is based on an approximation of an integral. A low number of draws lead to a poor approximation of this integral. That can lead to a situation in which the log-likelihood of the estimated model with, e.g. 100 draws is higher than the log-likelihood with 500 draws. It does not mean that we should use 100 draws, it just reflects a poor approximation of the integral. For a low number of draws, the log-likelihood of the estimated model can differ markedly, but the increase of draws usually leads to a stabilisation of the log-likelihood. We can even find models that converge with a low number of draws but do not converge with a high number of draws. This indicates an identification problem of the model that must be solved and that we cannot trust the results with a low number of draws. In the specification search stage of our research, we usually estimate different variations of our model and to lower the estimation cost of numerous preliminary models we set a low number of draws. This is also an incorrect approach as a low number of draws can lead to an incorrect specification decision. All the models we estimate in our specification search must be estimated with a sufficiently high number of draws.

Czajkowski and Budziński (2019) provide a systematic comparison of pseudo-random, Halton, Sobol and Modified Latin Hypercube Sampling draws under a wide set of experimental conditions in terms of experimental designs, the number of individuals (400–1,200) and the number of choice tasks per individual (4–12). Based on a Monte Carlo simulation, they demonstrate the extent of the simulation error resulting from using 100 up to 1,000,000 draws. They show that a scrambled Sobol sequence results in the lowest simulation error of all the simulation methods compared, irrespective of the experimental conditions, with Halton draws a close second.

Czajkowski and Budziński (2019) propose guidelines regarding how many draws are "enough" for the required precision level. Their measure is based on 95% confidence that log-likelihoods do not lead to simulation-driven erroneous inference and that parameter estimates are within 5% of their true values for all experimental settings considered. They find that as the number of observations increases, so do the absolute levels of log-likelihood, and the minimum number of draws for the required precision level. Conversely, in the case of parameter estimates, the reverse relationship is observed—increasing the number of observations reduces the number of draws required for a given precision level.

Overall, Czajkowski and Budziński (2019) show that satisfying these precision criteria depends on the number of observations and may require using over 2,000 *Sobol* draws in the case of 5-attribute designs and over 25,000 *Sobol* draws in the case of 10-attribute designs. It is also recommended to verify if the results are stable with respect to an increase in the number of draws.

References

Adamowicz W, Boxall P, Williams M, Louviere J (1998) Stated preference approaches for measuring passive use values: choice experiments and contingent valuation. Am J Agr Econ 80:64–75. https://doi.org/10.2307/3180269

Ahtiainen H, Pouta E, Artell J (2015) Modelling asymmetric preferences for water quality in choice experiments with individual-specific status quo alternatives. Water Resour Econ 12:1–13. https://doi.org/10.1016/j.wre.2015.10.003

Bahamonde-Birke FJ, Kunert U, Link H, Ortúzar J de D (2017) About attitudes and perceptions: finding the proper way to consider latent variables in discrete choice models. Transportation 44:475–493. https://doi.org/10.1007/s11116-015-9663-5

Batley R, Ibáñez Rivas JN (2013) Applied welfare economics with discrete choice models: implications of theory for empirical specification. In: Hess S, Daly A (eds) Choice Modelling. Edward Elgar Publishing, pp 144–171

Bech M, Gyrd-Hansen D (2005) Effects coding in discrete choice experiments. Health Econ 14:1079–1083. https://doi.org/10.1002/hec.984

Bhat CR (2003) Simulation estimation of mixed discrete choice models using randomized and scrambled Halton sequences. Transp Res Part B Methodol 37:837–855. https://doi.org/10.1016/S0191-2615(02)00090-5

Bhat CR (2001) Quasi-random maximum simulated likelihood estimation of the mixed multinomial logit model. Transp Res Part B Methodol 35:677–693. https://doi.org/10.1016/S0191-2615(00)00014-X

Bhat CR, Sidharthan R (2011) A simulation evaluation of the maximum approximate composite marginal likelihood (MACML) estimator for mixed multinomial probit models. Transp Res Part B Methodol 45:940–953. https://doi.org/10.1016/j.trb.2011.04.006

Bierlaire M (2020) Biogeme. https://biogeme.epfl.ch/. Accessed 21 May 2020

Borriello A, Rose JM (2019) Global versus localised attitudinal responses in discrete choice. Transportation. https://doi.org/10.1007/s11116-019-10045-3

Boyce C, Czajkowski M, Hanley N (2019) Personality and economic choices. J Environ Econ Manag 94:82–100. https://doi.org/10.1016/j.jeem.2018.12.004

Brownstone D, Train K (1998) Forecasting new product penetration with flexible substitution patterns. J Econometrics 89:109–129

Budziński W, Czajkowski M (2018) Hybrid choice models vs. endogeneity of indicator variables: a Monte Carlo investigation. Faculty of Economic Sciences, University of Warsaw

Burton M (2018) Model invariance when estimating random parameters with categorical variables. Working Paper 1804, Agricultural and Resource Economics, The University of Western Australia, Crawley, Australia.

Campbell D, Hensher DA, Scarpa R (2014) Bounding WTP distributions to reflect the "actual" consideration set. J Choice Model 11:4–15. https://doi.org/10.1016/j.jocm.2014.02.004

Carson RT, Czajkowski M (2019) A new baseline model for estimating willingness to pay from discrete choice models. J Environ Econ Manage 95:57–61. https://doi.org/10.1016/j.jeem.2019.03.003

Chiou L, Walker JL (2007) Masking identification of discrete choice models under simulation methods. J Econometrics 141:683–703. https://doi.org/10.1016/j.jeconom.2006.10.012

Chorus CG, Kroesen M (2014) On the (im-)possibility of deriving transport policy implications from hybrid choice models. Transp Policy 36:217–222. https://doi.org/10.1016/j.tranpol.2014.09.001

Czajkowski M, Budziński W (2019) Simulation error in maximum likelihood estimation of discrete choice models. J Choice Model 31:73–85. https://doi.org/10.1016/j.jocm.2019.04.003

Czajkowski M, Hanley N, Nyborg K (2017) Social norms, morals and self-interest as determinants of pro-environment behaviours: the case of household recycling. Environ Resource Econ 66:647–670. https://doi.org/10.1007/s10640-015-9964-3

Czajkowski M, Vossler CA, Budziński W et al (2017) Addressing empirical challenges related to the incentive compatibility of stated preferences methods. J Econ Behav Organ 142:47–63. https://doi.org/10.1016/j.jebo.2017.07.023

Daly A, Dekker T, Hess S (2016) Dummy coding vs effects coding for categorical variables: clarifications and extensions. J Choice Model. https://doi.org/10.1016/j.jocm.2016.09.005

Daly A, Hess S, de Jong G (2012) Calculating errors for measures derived from choice modelling estimates. Transp Res Part B Methodol 46:333–341. https://doi.org/10.1016/j.trb.2011.10.008

Daly A, Hess S, Train K (2012) Assuring finite moments for willingness to pay in random coefficient models. Transportation 39:19–31. https://doi.org/10.1007/s11116-011-9331-3

Dekker T (2016) Asymmetric triangular mixing densities for mixed logit models. J Choice Model 21:48–55. https://doi.org/10.1016/j.jocm.2016.09.006

Dekker T, Hess S, Brouwer R, Hofkes M (2016) Decision uncertainty in multi-attribute stated preference studies. Resource Energy Econ 43:57–73. https://doi.org/10.1016/j.reseneeco.2015.11.002

Farsi M (2010) Risk aversion and willingness to pay for energy efficient systems in rental apartments. Energy Policy 38:3078–3088. https://doi.org/10.1016/j.enpol.2010.01.048

References

Fiebig DG, Keane MP, Louviere J, Wasi N (2010) The generalized multinomial logit model: accounting for scale and coefficient heterogeneity. Market Sci 29:393–421. https://doi.org/10.1287/mksc.1090.0508

Fosgerau M, Bierlaire M (2007) A practical test for the choice of mixing distribution in discrete choice models. Transp Res B Methodol 41:784–794. https://doi.org/10.1016/j.trb.2007.01.002

Fosgerau M, Mabit SL (2013) Easy and flexible mixture distributions. Econ Lett 120:206–210. https://doi.org/10.1016/j.econlet.2013.03.050

Glenk K (2011) Using local knowledge to model asymmetric preference formation in willingness to pay for environmental services. J Environ Manage 92:531–541. https://doi.org/10.1016/j.jenvman.2010.09.003

Glenk K, Colombo S (2013) Modelling outcome-related risk in choice experiments. Aust J Agric Resource Econ 57:559–578. https://doi.org/10.1111/1467-8489.12012

Glenk K, Lago M, Moran D (2011) Public preferences for water quality improvements: implications for the implementation of the EC Water Framework Directive in Scotland. Water Policy 13:645–662. https://doi.org/10.2166/wp.2011.060

Greene WH (2017) Econometric analysis, 8th edn. Pearson, New York, NY

Greene WH, Hensher DA (2003) A latent class model for discrete choice analysis: contrasts with mixed logit. Transp Res Part B Methodol 37:681–698. https://doi.org/10.1016/S0191-2615(02)00046-2

Greene WH, Hensher DA (2013) Revealing additional dimensions of preference heterogeneity in a latent class mixed multinomial logit model. Appl Econ 45:1897–1902. https://doi.org/10.1080/00036846.2011.650325

Greene WH, Hensher DA (2010) Does scale heterogeneity across individuals matter? An empirical assessment of alternative logit models. Transportation 37:413–428. https://doi.org/10.1007/s11116-010-9259-z

Guevara CA, Tirachini A, Hurtubia R, Dekker T (2018) Correcting for endogeneity due to omitted crowding in public transport choice using the Multiple Indicator Solution (MIS) method. Transp Res Part A: Policy Pract. https://doi.org/10.1016/j.tra.2018.10.030

Hanemann WM (1984) Discrete/continuous models of consumer demand. Econometrica 52:541–561

Hensher DA, Greene WH (2003) The mixed logit model: the state of practice. Transportation 30:133–176. https://doi.org/10.1023/A:1022558715350

Hess S (2014) Latent class structures: taste heterogeneity and beyond. In: Hess S, Daly A (eds) Handbook of choice modelling. Edward Elgar Publishing, Cheltenham, UK, pp 311–329

Hess S, Beharry-Borg N (2012) Accounting for latent attitudes in willingness-to-pay studies: the case of coastal water quality improvements in Tobago. Environ Resource Econ 52:109–131. https://doi.org/10.1007/s10640-011-9522-6

Hess S, Rose JM (2009) Allowing for intra-respondent variations in coefficients estimated on repeated choice data. Transp Res B Methodol 43:708–719. https://doi.org/10.1016/j.trb.2009.01.007

Hess S, Rose JM (2012) Can scale and coefficient heterogeneity be separated in random coefficients models? Transportation 39:1225–1239. https://doi.org/10.1007/s11116-012-9394-9

Hess S, Rose JM, Polak J (2010) Non-trading, lexicographic and inconsistent behaviour in stated choice data. Transp Res D Transp Environ 15:405–417. https://doi.org/10.1016/j.trd.2010.04.008

Hess S, Train K (2017) Correlation and scale in mixed logit models. J Choice Model 23:1–8. https://doi.org/10.1016/j.jocm.2017.03.001

Hess S, Train KE, Polak JW (2006) On the use of a Modified Latin Hypercube Sampling (MLHS) method in the estimation of a Mixed Logit Model for vehicle choice. Transp Res B Methodol 40:147–163. https://doi.org/10.1016/j.trb.2004.10.005

Hole AR, Yoo HI (2017) The use of heuristic optimization algorithms to facilitate maximum simulated likelihood estimation of random parameter logit models. J Roy Stat Soc: Ser C (Appl Stat) 66:997–1013. https://doi.org/10.1111/rssc.12209

Hoyos D, Mariel P, Hess S (2015) Incorporating environmental attitudes in discrete choice models: an exploration of the utility of the awareness of consequences scale. Sci Total Environ 505:1100–1111. https://doi.org/10.1016/j.scitotenv.2014.10.066

Huber J, Train K (2001) On the similarity of classical and Bayesian estimates of individual mean partworths. Market Lett 12:259–269. https://doi.org/10.1023/A:1011120928698

Karlõševa A, Nõmmann S, Nõmmann T et al (2016) Marine trade-offs: comparing the benefits of off-shore wind farms and marine protected areas. Energy Econ 55:127–134. https://doi.org/10.1016/j.eneco.2015.12.022

Keane M, Wasi N (2013) Comparing alternative models of heterogeneity in consumer choice behavior. J Appl Econometrics 28:1018–1045. https://doi.org/10.1002/jae.2304

Lanz B, Provins A, Bateman IJ et al (2010) Investigating willingness to pay–willingness to accept asymmetry in Choice experiments. In: Hess S, Daly A (eds) Choice modelling: the state-of-the-art and the state-of-practice, pp 517–541

Long JS (1997) Regression models for categorical and limited dependent variables, 1st edn. Sage, Thousand Oaks

Mariel P, De Ayala A, Hoyos D, Abdullah S (2013) Selecting random parameters in discrete choice experiment for environmental valuation: a simulation experiment. J Choice Model 7:44–57. https://doi.org/10.1016/j.jocm.2013.04.008

Mariel P, Hoyos D, Artabe A, Guevara CA (2018) A multiple indicator solution approach to endogeneity in discrete-choice models for environmental valuation. Sci Total Environ 633:967–980. https://doi.org/10.1016/j.scitotenv.2018.03.254

Mariel P, Meyerhoff J (2016) Hybrid discrete choice models: gained insights versus increasing effort. Sci Total Environ 568:433–443. https://doi.org/10.1016/j.scitotenv.2016.06.019

Mariel P, Meyerhoff J (2018) A more flexible model or simply more effort? On the use of correlated random parameters in applied choice studies. Ecol Econ 154:419–429. https://doi.org/10.1016/j.ecolecon.2018.08.020

McCullough BD, Vinod HD (2003) Verifying the solution from a nonlinear solver: a case study. Am Econ Rev 93:873–892. https://doi.org/10.1257/000282803322157133

McFadden D (1974) Conditional logit analysis of qualitative choice behaviour. In: Zarembka P (ed) Academic Press, New York, pp 105–142

McFadden D, Train K (2000) Mixed MNL models for discrete response. J Appl Econometrics 15:447–470. https://doi.org/10.1002/1099-1255(200009/10)15:5%3c447::AID-JAE570%3e3.0.CO;2-1

Mebane WR, Sekhon JS (2011) Genetic Optimization Using Derivatives: the rgenoud Package for R. J Stat Softw 42:1–26. https://doi.org/10.18637/jss.v042.i11

Revelt D, Train K (1998) Mixed Logit with repeated choices: households' choices of appliance efficiency level. Rev Econ Stat 80:647–657. https://doi.org/10.1162/003465398557735

Sagebiel J, Glenk K, Meyerhoff J (2017) Spatially explicit demand for afforestation. Forest Policy Econ 78:190–199. https://doi.org/10.1016/j.forpol.2017.01.021

Scarpa R, Ferrini S, Willis K (2005) Performance of error component models for status-quo effects in choice experiments. In: Scarpa R, Alberini A (eds) Applications of simulation methods in environmental and resource economics. Springer, Netherlands, Dordrecht, pp 247–273

Scarpa R, Thiene M, Marangon F (2008a) Using flexible taste distributions to value collective reputation for environmentally friendly production methods. Can J Agric Econ 56:145–162. https://doi.org/10.1111/j.1744-7976.2008.00122.x

Scarpa R, Thiene M, Train K (2008b) Utility in willingness to pay space: a tool to address confounding random scale effects in destination choice to the Alps. Am J Agr Econ 90:994–1010. https://doi.org/10.1111/j.1467-8276.2008.01155.x

Small K, Rosen H (1981) applied welfare economics with discrete choice models. Econometrica 49:105–130

Stathopoulos A, Hess S (2011) Referencing, gains-losses asymmetry and non-linear sensitivities in commuter decisions: one size does not fit all! Working Papers 0511. CREI Università degli Studi Roma Tre

References

Train K (2016) Mixed logit with a flexible mixing distribution. J Choice Model 19:40–53. https://doi.org/10.1016/j.jocm.2016.07.004

Train K (2009) Discrete choice methods with simulation, 2nd edn. Cambridge University Press, New York

Train K, Sonnier G (2005) Mixed logit with bounded distributions of correlated partworths. In: Scarpa R, Alberini A (eds) Springer. The Netherlands, Dordrecht, pp 1–16

Train K, Weeks M (2005) Discrete choice models in preference space and willingness-to-pay space. In: Scarpa R, Alberini A (eds) Springer. The Netherlands, Dordrecht, pp 1–16

Tuhkanen H, Piirsalu E, Nõmmann T et al (2016) Valuing the benefits of improved marine environmental quality under multiple stressors. Sci Total Environ 551–552:367–375. https://doi.org/10.1016/j.scitotenv.2016.02.011

Vij A, Walker JL (2016) How, when and why integrated choice and latent variable models are latently useful. Transp Res B Methodol 90:192–217. https://doi.org/10.1016/j.trb.2016.04.021

Walker JL, Ben-Akiva M, Bolduc D (2007) Identification of parameters in normal error component logit-mixture (NECLM) models. J Appl Econ 22:1095–1125. https://doi.org/10.1002/jae.971

Wang X, Kockelman KM (2006) Tracking Land cover change in mixed logit model: recognizing temporal and spatial effects. Transp Res Rec 1977:112–120. https://doi.org/10.1177/0361198106197700114

Zawojska E, Bartczak A, Czajkowski M (2019) Disentangling the effects of policy and payment consequentiality and risk attitudes on stated preferences. J Environ Econ Manag 93:63–84. https://doi.org/10.1016/j.jeem.2018.11.007

Open Access This chapter is licensed under the terms of the Creative Commons Attribution 4.0 International License (http://creativecommons.org/licenses/by/4.0/), which permits use, sharing, adaptation, distribution and reproduction in any medium or format, as long as you give appropriate credit to the original author(s) and the source, provide a link to the Creative Commons license and indicate if changes were made.

The images or other third party material in this chapter are included in the chapter's Creative Commons license, unless indicated otherwise in a credit line to the material. If material is not included in the chapter's Creative Commons license and your intended use is not permitted by statutory regulation or exceeds the permitted use, you will need to obtain permission directly from the copyright holder.

Chapter 6
Econometric Modelling: Extensions

Abstract This chapter is devoted to advanced issues of econometric modelling. The topics covered are, among others, models in willingness to pay space, the meaning of scale heterogeneity in discrete choice models and the application of various information processing rules such as random regret minimisation or attribute non-attendance. Other topics are anchoring and learning effects when respondents move through a sequence of choice tasks as well as different information processing strategies such as lexicographic preferences or choices based on elimination-by-aspects.

6.1 WTP-Space Versus Preference Space

The estimation of WTP is one of the main outcomes of DCE studies. WTP measures are crucial, as they inform policy makers with regard the values people attach to goods and/or services which, in turn, can help the former tailor pricing (Hanley et al. 2003) and they can be typically used in cost–benefit analyses.

Computation of WTP values, however, is not always straightforward (see also Sects. 5.4 and 5.5). This is because WTP estimates are typically calculated as the ratio of two coefficients (with the cost coefficient being the denominator), which, in the case of models with random parameters, leads to a ratio of two distributions. In the case of WTP estimates derived from a RP-MXL, the estimates depend on the distributional assumptions imposed by the researcher for each of the coefficients. Conventional utility specifications often imply implausible distributions of welfare estimates, given that the typical estimate of WTP is retrieved by the ratio of two distributed coefficient estimates. The problem is that values of the denominator that are close to zero (most likely within standard distributions such as the log-normal) cause the ratio to be extremely large, thereby implying an unrealistic derived distribution of WTP due to a long upper tail (Train and Weeks 2005; Scarpa et al. 2008).

Some attempts to address this problem rely on strong and generally unrealistic assumptions, such as imposing a fixed cost coefficient: when the coefficient of an attribute is distributed normally, this implies that the WTP for that attribute is also normally distributed, as the two distributions take the same form. This assumption

© The Author(s) 2021
P. Mariel et al., *Environmental Valuation with Discrete Choice Experiments*,
SpringerBriefs in Economics, https://doi.org/10.1007/978-3-030-62669-3_6

cannot be universally recommended for general application, although it may be appropriate in some cases (Hole and Kolstad 2012). As Train and Weeks (2005) stressed, assuming a fixed price coefficient implies that the standard deviation of unobserved utility (i.e. the scale parameter) is the same for all observations, thereby implying that the marginal utility of money is the same for each respondent. In fact, the scale parameter can—and in many situations clearly does—vary randomly over observations. Hence, one increasingly adopted alternative is the estimation of models in which the distribution of the welfare measure is modelled directly. In the traditional framework, models parameterised in coefficient distributions are called "models in preference space", whereas models parameterised in WTP distributions are "models in WTP space". In other words, the parameters are the (marginal) WTP for each attribute rather than the utility coefficient of each attribute. The first examples of models in WTP space are provided by Cameron and James (1987) and Cameron (1988).

For random coefficient models, the issue of which parameterisation to use is more complex and potentially more important, as noted by Train and Weeks (2005). The latter are the seminal papers of parametrisation in WTP space, Scarpa et al. (2008) provided the first application in environmental economics. Mutually compatible distributions for coefficients and WTPs can be specified either way but differ in their convenience for assigning parameter distributions and imposing constraints on these distributions.

According to (1.4) and to (1.5), the utility of respondent n for alternative j in choice occasion t is specified in the WTP-space (Train and Weeks 2005) as:

$$U_{njt}^* = \alpha_n^* \left(\omega_n x'_{njt} - p_{njt} \right) + \varepsilon_{njt}$$

where α_n^* is the price coefficient/scale parameter, ω_n is a conformable vector of marginal WTPs for each non-monetary attribute and p_{njt} is the cost attribute.

So the question then becomes: Is it better to use preference space or WTP space? Train and Weeks (2005) compare models using normal and log-normal distributions in preference space with those using normal and log-normal distributions in WTP space. Both studies found that models in preference space fit the within-sample data better than models in WTP space using different data sets. Both studies also found that distributions of WTP derived from estimated models in preference space have unreasonably large variances. Models in preference space imply that large proportions of respondents will pay unreasonably large sums to obtain/avoid extra units of non-price attributes. Models in WTP space exhibited smaller variances for WTP, implying smaller proportions of very large WTP values. Similar results were obtained by following previous studies (e.g. Hole and Kolstad 2012). Some studies, however, found models in WTP space that outperform models in preferences space also in terms of goodness of fit (Scarpa et al. 2008; Bae and Rishi 2018; Waldman and Richardson 2018). Overall, the accumulated empirical evidence suggests that models in WTP space yield a more reliable estimation of WTP space value, while there is no conclusive evidence about which model parametrisation performs better in terms of data fit. The adoption of models in preference or WTP space should therefore be evaluated according to the empirical case and to the purpose or the study (Hess and Rose 2012). Sensitivity testing is also recommended when choosing between preference and WTP space models (Hole and Kolstad 2012). Hypotheses regarding the WTP distributions can be tested directly by imposing restrictions on the distribution (i.e. the mean or the standard deviation) in the estimation and a subsequent likelihood-ratio test of the unrestricted and the restricted model (Thiene and Scarpa 2009). Importantly, when the goal is to obtain WTP measures to be used for policy purposes, parametrisation in WTP space seems to be the best option.

Models in WTP space, which might have convergence issues, can be estimated with several software commonly used in choice models, such as Biogeme (Bierlaire 2020), R (Sarrias and Daziano 2017; Hess and Palma 2019) or Stata by means of the codes provided by Hole (2020), and the DCE package for Matlab (Czajkowski 2020).

6.2 Scale Heterogeneity

The RUM assumes that latent utility consists of a deterministic part and a random error term (see Sect. 1.2). According to Eq. (1.3), the utility U_{njt} is decomposed into $V_{njt} + \varepsilon_{njt}$, where V_{njt} is the deterministic, quantifiable proportion of utility including both observables of the alternatives (the choice attributes) and of the individuals (age, gender, income, etc.) and ε_{njt} is the unobservable or random part associated with the utility. A RUM model requires an assumption about the distribution of these random effects. The scale parameter, which is by definition part of a RUM model, expresses the relationship between the observable and the random component as part of the overall latent utility. They are inversely related to the variance of the random component and cannot be separately identified from taste parameters generally denoted as β.

If the utility of all alternatives is multiplied by a constant, the alternative with the highest utility does not change. To take this fact into account, the scale of the utility must be normalised. As mentioned in Sect. 1.2, the model (1.4)

$$U_{njt} = V_{njt} + \varepsilon_{njt} = x'_{njt}\beta + \varepsilon_{njt}$$

is equivalent to (1.5)

$$U^*_{njt} = \lambda V_{njt} + \lambda \varepsilon_{njt} = x'_{njt}(\lambda\beta) + \lambda\varepsilon_{njt},$$

where the scale parameter is denoted as λ. Scale then describes the relationship between the observable and the random component of utility. If scale is equal across individuals and thus the same within a given data set, it does not impact on the relationships between utilities.

Normalising the scale of utility is usually achieved through normalising the variance of the error terms (see Sect. 1.2). The error variance, however, can differ across respondents and data sources, for example. Combining different data sets therefore requires us to control for scale differences as identical utility specifications from different data sources with unequal variance will differ in magnitude (Swait and Louviere 1993). Scale heterogeneity, and thus the variance of the error term, might not only differ among data sets but also among respondents within a data set. Given that scale describes the relationship between factors included in the model and factors not included in the model, it might be interpreted as an indicator for choice consistency. The variance of the random error component could indicate whether respondents made more deterministic or more random choices, with a higher error variance indicating less consistent choices. Examples for applications using this approach are, among many others, studies concerned with the effects of choice task complexity (e.g. Carlsson and Martinsson 2008b), of preference uncertainty (e.g. Uggeldahl et al. 2016) or of learning effects when respondent move through the sequence of choice tasks (e.g. Carlsson et al. 2012; Czajkowski et al. 2014) or anchoring and learning effects due to instructional choice sets (Ladenburg and Olsen 2008; Meyerhoff and Glenk 2015).

All these approaches are based on the specific assumption that the observed simultaneous correlation between all attributes is a result of scale heterogeneity. However, as noted by Hess and Rose (2012) and Hess and Train (2017), correlations among coefficients can have various sources, and scale heterogeneity is only one of them. If models are constrained in such a way that scale heterogeneity should come out as a separate parameter, they are also likely to pick up other forms of correlation and it is not possible, as already said, to separate them.

Two conclusions can be drawn from this. Firstly, it is important to check carefully whether scale heterogeneity is a valid indicator for what the analyst wishes to investigate given that it may pick up more than one source of correlation. Comparing scale parameters across exogenously determined groups might be an indicator for differences in the choice behaviour of the groups, but the interpretation has to account for the restriction the analyst imposed on his or her model. Secondly, after running basic MNL models to become familiar with the data, the next step could be to proceed with the analysis of the most flexible model specification (see Sect. 5.3). Depending on the model specification, a RP-MXL with a full random utility coefficient covariance matrix can account for correlations due to a behavioural phenomena as well as scale heterogeneity (Hess and Train 2017). Given the results of this model, the analyst might subsequently impose restrictions.

An important question in applied research is often whether the restrictions lead to different welfare measures. Thus testing welfare measures resulting from models with full and restricted covariance can be informative. Mariel and Meyerhoff (2018), for example, have not found significant differences between an unrestricted (accounting for scale heterogeneity) and a restricted (not accounting for scale heterogeneity) RP-MXL. This finding, of course, cannot be generalised as it might be data specific.

6.3 Information Processing Strategies

DCE is based on the economic theory of consumer behaviour (McFadden 1974), which posits three axioms about an individual's preferences: they are complete, monotonic and continuous. Continuity of preferences implies that individuals use compensatory decision-making processes, that is, they take into account all the available information to make their decisions. Typically, in a DCE, this implies that respondents make trade-offs between the levels of each attribute to choose their preferred alternative. However, in practice individuals often lack both the ability and the cognitive resources to evaluate all the information provided to them (Cameron and DeShazo 2010). For this reason, it has been argued that individuals behave in a rationally adaptive manner by seeking to minimise their cognitive efforts while at the same time aiming to maximise their benefits when making choices (DeShazo and Fermo 2004). For instance, people may not have well-defined preferences, but may construct them at the moment of the choice occasion. Moreover, rather than using a fixed decision strategy in all choice occasions, individuals may adopt different strategies in different situations. Often such strategies imply selective use of information and avoidance of trade-offs (Chater et al. 2003). Accounting for these aspects is important in DCE applications, as incongruency between DCE modelling assumptions and actual choice behaviour can lead to biased results and inaccurate forecasts (Hensher 2006). For this reason, a rapidly increasing body of literature deals with the investigation of information processing strategies that individuals adopt when making choices.

The study of information processing strategies is rooted in psychological theories of choice that assume a dual-phase model of the decision-making process (Kahneman and Tversky 1979; Thaler 1999). The first phase relates to the editing of the problem, whereas the second relates to the evaluation of the edited problem. The main function of the editing operations is to organise and reformulate the alternatives in order to reduce the amount of information to be processed and thus simplify choices (Kahneman and Tversky 1979). The main function of the evaluation operations is to select the preferred alternative (Hess and Hensher 2010). The editing phase often involves the adoption of heuristic strategies that determine the way in which information is processed to produce the choice outcome. A heuristic is a strategy that mainly, although not exclusively, consists of ignoring part of the information, with the purpose of making decisions more quickly and with less cognitive effort (Gigerenzer and Gaissmaier 2011). The adoption of heuristics strategies can be influenced by the cognitive ability of the respondent, his/her attitudes and believes, his/her knowledge of the item to be evaluated and socio-demographic characteristics (Deshazo and Fermo 2002). Yet, processing strategies, while important for setting up correct econometric models, are not specific to DCE or SP surveys, as people use these quite often in real life.

One of the information processing strategies most commonly investigated in the DCE literature is the so-called attribute non-attendance (ANA), which refers to respondents ignoring certain attributes when making their choices

(Hensher et al. 2006). ANA will be described in detail in Sect. 6.5. Other strategies that have received attention in the DCE literature are: (i) lexicographic preferences; (ii) elimination-by-aspects or selection-by-aspects; (iii) majority of confirming dimensions.

Lexicographic preferences have been commonly investigated in DCE studies (Sælensminde 2006; Campbell et al. 2008; Rose et al. 2013). Individuals that adopt such a strategy rank the attributes from the most to the least important and make their choices based solely on the levels of the most important one(s) (Foster and Mourato 2002). Lexicographic preferences violate the continuity axiom of the neoclassical framework and empirical studies suggest that this strategy has a significant impact on the results obtained from discrete choice models, i.e. biased WTP values (Campbell et al. 2008; Rose et al. 2013). The adoption of this strategy seems to be influenced by the design of the study and by the respondents' characteristics. For example, Sælensminde (2006) found that individuals with a relatively high level of education are less likely to adopt lexicographic behaviour.

Another common information processing strategy is the elimination-by-aspects heuristic. When this heuristic is applied, individuals gradually reduce the number of alternatives in a choice set, by eliminating those that include an undesirable aspect. For example, respondents may eliminate alternatives that are deemed too expensive, as for some of them cost is a key attribute (Campbell et al. 2014). One alternative is evaluated at time until a limited number of alternatives remain in the choice task and the choice requires lower cognitive effort. Individual motivations and/or goals (also known as antecedent volitions, as they antecede and direct decision-making process) may lead respondents to reduce and select choice sets (Thiene et al. 2017). Several DCE studies (Campbell et al. 2014; Erdem et al. 2014; Daniel et al. 2018) found evidence of the adoption of such a heuristic in empirical applications and highlight the importance of accounting for it in the econometric analysis. Daniel et al. (2018), for example, found that WTP values are overestimated when the adoption of this strategy is not taken into account.

Selection-by-aspects is a heuristic akin to elimination-by-aspects: in this case, rather than excluding alternatives with undesirable traits, individuals form choice tasks which include only alternatives with desirable ones (e.g. high level for an important attribute). Finally, under the majority of confirming dimensions heuristics (Russo and Dosher 1983), respondents compare alternatives in pairs, rather than evaluating all of them simultaneously. The "winning alternative" is then compared to another one until the overall preferred alternative is identified. Hensher and Collins (2011) and Leong and Hensher (2012) provide corroborating evidence of the adoption of such a strategy in DCE studies.

While the adoption of heuristics depends on an individual's characteristics and cognitive ability, there is corroborating evidence that their use also depends on the design of the DCE (Mørkbak et al. 2014; Campbell et al. 2018). Heuristics have been found more likely to be adopted when the DCE exercise requires substantial cognitive effort, for example, due to a large number of attributes, levels and alternatives (Collins and Hensher 2015). As such, accounting for heuristics is particularly advisable in empirical applications that require complex scenarios in order to accurately describe the good/service under evaluation. From a practical viewpoint: (i) the application of the above-applied information strategies is closely related to the definition of the choice tasks, so careful work with a focus group, rigorous preparation of the choice task and piloting can partially help avoid them; (ii) as the list of heuristic strategies is quite long, we will focus on one example, ANA, particularly relevant for DCE (see Sect. 6.5).

6.4 Random Regret Minimisation—An Alternative to Utility Maximisation

RRM has been introduced by Chorus et al. (2008) as an alternative to the RUM paradigm commonly used in discrete choice studies. RRM assumes that individuals choose between alternatives with the goal of avoiding the situation in which a non-chosen alternative turns out to be better than the chosen one, i.e. a choice that the individual would regret. Hence, the individual is assumed to minimise regret rather than to maximise utility (Chorus 2012). From an analytical point of view, the level of anticipated random regret is composed of an *i.i.d.* random error, which represents unobserved heterogeneity in regret, and a systematic regret component. Systematic regret is given by the sum of all binary regrets that arise from the comparison between an alternative and each of the other alternatives.

A central question in RRM literature has been whether and under which conditions RRM can be used as an alternative to the RUM. Chorus et al. (2014) carried out a meta-analysis on 21 studies to explore "to what extent, when and how RRM can form a viable addition to the consumer choice modeller's toolkit". Their analysis highlights how neither of the two paradigms performs consistently better than the other, and how the differences in goodness of fit are in most cases small. Interestingly, the authors note that there are some specific empirical contexts in which a paradigm performs frequently better than the other. They highlight how regret plays an important role when the choice is either considered difficult and/or important for the individuals, when they feel they will need to justify their choice to other people and when they are not familiar with the good or service under analysis. For example, RRM has been found to perform better than RUM in contexts such as car type and energy choices (Boeri and Longo 2017), whereas choices are often more consistent with RUM in other contexts such as leisure time activities (Thiene et al. 2012). It is also important to note that while often performing similarly in terms of model fit, several studies found that the two paradigms substantially differ in terms of forecasting and prediction of market shares for products or services (Chorus et al. 2014; van Cranenburgh and Chorus 2017). For this reason, the choice of paradigm may have a substantial practical impact. Some studies also found evidence that the relative performance of the two paradigms is influenced by experimental design features. For example, the effect of the opt-out option on RRM and RUM performance has received attention in the literature. Chorus (2012) and Thiene et al. (2012) suggest RRM may be less suitable for the analysis of choices where an opt-out alternative is presented, since this alternative cannot be compared to other alternatives at the attribute level and as such regret cannot be experienced. Hess et al. (2014) further investigate such effects and conclude that not only does the presence of an opt-out option affect the model's performance, but also the way in which the option is presented. In particular, their results suggest that RRM performs worse when the opt-out option is framed as a "none of these", while the RUM performs worse when it is framed as an "indifferent" option. Moreover, van Cranenburgh et al. (2018) found that RUM-efficient designs can be statistically highly inefficient in cases where RRM better represents an individual's choice behaviour, and vice versa. A possible alternative to the choice of a RUM- or RRM-based choice model is the adoption of hybrid models where both decision processes co-exist in the same population. Hess et al. (2012) proposed the use of a latent class approach where different decision rules are used in different classes. Boeri et al. (2014) add to this, by allowing for random taste heterogeneity within each behavioural class. Chorus et al. (2013), however, proposed a MXL where instead of distinguishing sub-groups of respondents, a subset of attributes is subject to RUM, and another subset subject to RRM. Kim et al. (2017) incorporated a hybrid RUM–RRM model into an HCM framework. In most cases, these hybrid models perform better than models that assume the same rule of behaviour (RRM or RUM) for each attribute. Chorus et al. (2014), however, do not suggest the blind adoption of hybrid RUM–RRM models and rather suggest the adoption of the same practices outlined for the choice between pure RUM or RRM model (e.g. comparison of model fit or simultaneous estimation of different models). RRM models have some difficulties in deriving WTP measures, which is crucial as this is often one of the purposes in most environmental DCE applications, although recently relevant progress has been made (Dekker and Chorus 2018).

In terms of best practices, the following suggestions can be derived from the literature, which are for the most part in line with the indications of Chorus et al. (2014): (1) to choose RUM or RRM in contexts in which one of the paradigms often performs better than the other (e.g., RRM for car choices); (2) in the case of studies which specifically focus on RRM models, the formulation of the opt-out option (if present) and the type of experimental design should be carefully chosen; (3) to estimate both RUM and RRM models on a given dataset and then choose the model with the best fit for further analyses and the derivation of relevant output for policymakers (e.g. elasticities); and (4) to avoid choosing either of the two models, rather to implement them both simultaneously and then jointly use outcomes from RUM and RRM to construct a number of behavioural scenarios using either a RUM, RRM or hybrid RUM–RRM model.

A comprehensive website that, among other features, provides estimation codes for different random regret models (P-RRM model, μRRM model, the G-RRM model and various latent class models) and different software packages (Biogeme, Apollo R, Matlab, Latent Gold Choice) is van Cranenburgh (2020). Moreover, also available on this website is advice on how to generate decision rule robust experimental designs (see also van Cranenburgh et al. 2018 and van Cranenburgh and Collins 2019).

6.5 Attribute Non-attendance

As mentioned in Sect. 6.3, respondents do not necessarily consider all attributes within a choice set when making their choices. Non-attended attributes in the choice set imply non-compensatory behaviour: independently from the improvement of an attribute level—if the attribute itself is ignored by the respondent—then such an improvement will fail to compensate for a worsening in the levels of the other attributes. As a consequence, respondents using such a strategy raise a problem for neoclassical analysis as they cannot be represented by a conventional utility function (Hensher 2006). In the absence of continuity, there is no trade-off between two different attributes. Without a trade-off, there is no computable marginal rate of substitution and, crucially for non-market valuation, no computable WTP.

ANA may arise due to several reasons, such as an individual's attitudes (Balbontin et al. 2017), knowledge/familiarity with the attributes (Sandorf et al. 2017), task complexity (Weller et al. 2014; Collins and Hensher 2015), unrealism of the attribute's levels (i.e. respondents ignore an attribute because they feel the proposed levels are unattainable) and genuine disinterest towards an attribute (Alemu et al. 2013). Carlsson et al. (2010) and Campbell et al. (2008) found that ignoring ANA impacted model fits and welfare estimates.

The identification of ANA has been carried out with different methods in the literature. The two most common approaches are stated ANA and inferred ANA (Hensher 2006; Scarpa et al. 2009a, 2010). A third approach to identify ANA has been recently proposed, and it is based on eye-tracking. This has been referred as visual or revealed ANA (Balcombe et al. 2015).

The stated ANA approach involves asking respondents directly whether they ignored one or more attributes when making choices. This is usually done by including such a question in the survey specific questions after the choice scenarios. Several approaches have been proposed in the literature to inform discrete choice models with the answers to such questions. A common approach, described in Hensher et al. (2005) and then adopted by following studies (Hensher et al. 2007b; Kaye-Blake et al. 2009; Kragt 2013), is to specify choice models in which the coefficient of attributes that respondents state to have ignored is constrained to zero. Some authors have extended this kind of approach, by reducing the magnitude of ignored coefficients by means of shrinking parameters, instead of constraining them to zero (Alemu et al. 2013; Balcombe et al. 2014, 2015; Chalak et al. 2016; Hess and Hensher 2010). Alternative approaches involve (i) specifying error component models with different scale parameters for subsets of respondents that ignored different numbers of attributes (Campbell et al. 2008); (ii) estimating heteroskedastic MNL models that account for variance induced by ANA (Scarpa et al. 2010); (iii) estimating separate attributes coefficients for the group of respondents who stated they did not ignore the attributes and for those who stated they had (Hess and Hensher 2010; Scarpa et al. 2013). Another approach to modelling attribute decision rules involves the use of a hybrid choice modelling approach. Each individual question about attribute attendance is treated as a binary indicator variable that represents a latent variable (Hess and Hensher 2013).

Along with differences in how ANA information is incorporated in choice models, stated ANA approaches also differ in terms of how such information is collected. In particular, stated ANA can be divided into two forms: serial ANA and choice task ANA. In serial ANA, respondents are asked to report at the end of the sequence of choice tasks if they systematically ignored one or more attributes when making choices. Whereas, in the choice task ANA, such a question is asked after each choice task.

Scarpa et al. (2010) compared serial and choice task ANA and found that accounting for choice task ANA significantly improves model fit and yields more accurate marginal WTP estimates. Caputo et al. (2018) found similar results, and they suggest that respondents may not follow the same attribute processing strategies throughout the entire sequence of choice tasks. As such, they conclude that collecting ANA information at the choice task level may be more desirable than at the serial level.

Inferred ANA, however, consists of inferring ANA behaviour through the estimation of analytical models. This approach typically makes use of an equality-constrained latent class model where the classes, rather than latent preference groups, represent different attribute processing strategies and during estimation parameters are set to zero in specific classes to account for ignored attributes (Campbell et al. 2011; Caputo et al. 2013; Glenk et al. 2015; Hensher et al. 2012; Hensher and Greene 2010; Hole et al. 2013; Lagarde 2013; Scarpa et al. 2009b; Thiene et al. 2015), while they are constrained to be equal across classes when non-zero.

In most applications, estimated coefficients are assumed to take the same values across classes (Scarpa et al. 2009b; Hensher and Greene 2010; Campbell et al. 2011). Only a few studies have investigated preferences heterogeneity within ANA classes: Thiene et al. (2015) mixed ANA classes with preference classes, whereas Hess et al. (2013), Hensher et al. (2013) and Thiene et al. (2017) adopted a Latent Class-Random Parameters (LCRP-MXL) specification that accounts for both attribute non-attendance and continuous taste heterogeneity. Another method to infer ANA was proposed by Hess and Hensher (2010) which involves the estimation of the individual posterior conditional distributions of coefficients from a RP-MXL. In particular, the authors, as well as other studies employing this approach (e.g. Scarpa et al. 2013) retrieved the mean (μ) and the variance (σ) of such distributions and computed the ratio between them (σ/μ). When the ratio for an attribute is high (>2), it can be assumed that the respondent did not attend to it when making his/her choices.

Finally, the so-called visual or revealed ANA involves detecting ANA by means of eye-tracking technologies, which monitor the fixations and time spent on each attribute (Balcombe et al. 2015, 2016; Spinks and Mortimer 2016; Chavez et al. 2018). This approach, which seems very promising compared to the other two (Uggeldahl et al. 2017), has the advantage of retrieving information without eliciting them from respondents, providing a less biased measure than that retrieved from stated ANA (Balcombe et al. 2015). Data retrieved by using this approach are usually modelled as in the stated ANA approach, that is by estimating parameters that shrink the coefficients for non-attended attributes (Balcombe et al. 2015; Chavez et al. 2018). These studies found inconsistencies between stated and visual ANA and that models informed with both approaches had the best results in terms of statistical fit. Furthermore, authors found that the time spent on choice tasks tends to diminish during the sequence. In particular, Spinks and Mortimer (2016) found that the number of attributes ignored by each respondent can vary among choice tasks, therefore supporting the existence of differences between choice task level and serial non-attendance.

A central question in the ANA literature concerns which of the three approaches should be used to account for it. Several studies advocated the use of inferred ANA over stated ANA, due to some limitations with the latter approach. Some authors, in particular, questioned whether respondents' statements are reliable (Campbell and Lorimer 2009). Respondents may not answer follow-up questions completely truthfully for several reasons, such as social pressure to care about an attribute (especially when surveys are carried out by means of face-to-face interviews), or to consider all attributes as relevant (Balcombe et al. 2011). Yet, inferred ANA might suffer from other limitations, as for example, questionable assumptions in the model. Another issue with using respondents' statements is potential endogeneity bias that arises from conditioning a model on self-reported ANA (Hess and Hensher 2013). Several studies employed both the stated non-attendance and the inferred non-attendance approach (Hensher et al. 2007a; Hensher and Rose 2009; Campbell et al. 2011; Scarpa et al. 2013; Mørkbak et al. 2014). The overall finding is that results from inferred and stated ANA are inconsistent with each other, and that the inferred approach generally provides a better model fit. Mørkbak et al. (2014) highlight that ANA is not a problem for DCE only, as it is also present in real life and in incentivised settings.

Finally, another important question is whether there are some situations in which accounting for ANA is particularly advisable. Based on the evidence concerning underlying drivers of ANA behaviour, it seems especially important to account for it in studies with complex designs with, for example, high number of attributes and/or alternatives (Weller et al. 2014), in contexts in which a part of the population is unlikely to be very interested in certain attributes (e.g. categories of visitors in destination studies) and in cases in which some respondents are likely to have a low familiarity with some of the attributes. On the other hand, ANA seems to have a lower impact on choices in applications in which the target population is bound to be very knowledgeable about the good/service under evaluation (e.g. doctors for medicines attributes, Hole et al. 2013).

6.6 Anchoring and Learning Effects

Anchoring is a term used in psychology to describe the disproportionate influence on individuals that an initially presented value may have on their judgements (Tversky and Kahneman 1974). In the environmental valuation literature, anchoring or starting point bias refers to the concern that initial bids in a choice experiment may provide respondents facing unfamiliar environmental goods with an anchor that may bias the elicitation of their true preferences (Mitchell and Carson 1989). Although anchoring may be due to informative and non-informative information while starting point effects are always due to informative information, both concepts are usually treated indifferently in the literature (for more detailed discussion see Glenk et al. 2019).

Anchoring effects, as with other context effects found in the SP literature, have challenged the alleged stability and coherence of preferences, as assumed by microeconomic theory underlying DCE. In the context of DCE for the valuation of public goods, anchoring or starting point bias refers to the use of previous information (e.g. information provided by instructional choice sets or initial choice sets and cost bids) as reference points that affect subsequent choices and, accordingly, welfare estimates. The literature distinguishes two forms of anchoring or starting point effect: price vector anchoring effects, i.e. the effect on preferences of using different price or cost vectors; and starting point anchoring effects, i.e. the price used in the first choice set may influence respondents' preferences.

Evidence regarding the existence of anchoring effects in DCE is mixed: while some authors have found no evidence of preference instability after changing the range of prices used in a survey (Ohler et al. 2000; Ryan and Wordsworth 2000; Hanley et al. 2005), others have found that increasing the price levels had a significant upward effect on preferences and estimated WTP (Carlsson et al. 2007; Carlsson and Martinsson 2008a; Mørkbak et al. 2010). Although they may be present in many SP experiments, price vector effects have been found to be more likely to appear when involving non-use environmental goods (Burrows et al. 2017).

Ladenburg and Olsen (2008) find that certain groups of respondents are susceptible to starting point bias whereas others are not. Importantly, their results indicate that the impact of the starting point bias decays as respondents evaluate more and more choice sets. When faced with an unfamiliar choice situation, respondents are initially influenced by value questions, but progressing through a sequence of choice sets, they become more familiar with the choice situation and discover their own preferences, in line with the Discovered Preference Hypothesis (Braga and Starmer 2005). Learning and fatigue effects have also received specific attention (Campbell et al. 2015; Carlsson et al. 2012; Meyerhoff and Glenk 2015).

Careful survey design is a precondition for minimising biases in DCE. A clear description of the decision rule (i.e. the conditions under which the environmental good is provided) is crucial for minimising not only strategic behaviour (see Sect. 2.9), but for obtaining WTP estimates which are more internally consistent and less dependent on anchoring (Aravena et al. 2018). Randomisation of choice sets, attributes and alternatives is also recommended to reduce the impact of starting point effects (Glenk et al. 2019). Practitioners should also be aware that using multiple valuation questions through a sequence of choice sets might affect the consistency of elicited preferences. However, the recent literature has found learning effects in repetitive choice sets, given the unfamiliarity that respondents usually show when valuing environmental goods and services. So, the repetitive nature of choice tasks

6.6 Anchoring and Learning Effects

may indeed help respondents through a process of learning about their true preferences and provide more consistent parameter estimates (Bateman et al. 2008; Ladenburg and Olsen 2008; Brouwer et al. 2010).

References

Alemu MH, Mørkbak MR, Olsen SB, Jensen CL (2013) Attending to the reasons for attribute non-attendance in choice experiments. Environ Resource Econ 54:333–359. https://doi.org/10.1007/s10640-012-9597-8

Aravena C, Hutchinson WG, Carlsson F, Matthews DI (2018) Testing preference formation in learning design contingent valuation using advance information and repetitive treatments. Land Economics 94:284–301. https://doi.org/10.3368/le.94.2.284

Bae JH, Rishi M (2018) Increasing consumer participation rates for green pricing programs: a choice experiment for South Korea. Energy Econ 74:490–502. https://doi.org/10.1016/j.eneco.2018.06.027

Balbontin C, Hensher DA, Collins AT (2017) Integrating attribute non-attendance and value learning with risk attitudes and perceptual conditioning. Transp Res E Logist Transp Rev 97:172–191. https://doi.org/10.1016/j.tre.2016.11.002

Balcombe K, Bitzios M, Fraser I, Haddock-Fraser J (2014) Using attribute importance rankings within discrete Choice experiments: an application to valuing bread attributes. J Agric Econ 65:446–462. https://doi.org/10.1111/1477-9552.12051

Balcombe K, Burton M, Rigby D (2011) Skew and attribute non-attendance within the Bayesian mixed logit model. J Environ Econ Manag 62:446–461. https://doi.org/10.1016/j.jeem.2011.04.004

Balcombe K, Fraser I, Lowe B, Souza Monteiro D (2016) Information customization and food choice. Am J Agric Econ 98:54–73. https://doi.org/10.1093/ajae/aav033

Balcombe K, Fraser I, McSorley E (2015) Visual attention and attribute attendance in multi-attribute choice experiments. J Appl Econ 30:447–467. https://doi.org/10.1002/jae.2383

Bateman IJ, Burgess D, Hutchinson WG, Matthews DI (2008) Learning design contingent valuation (LDCV): NOAA guidelines, preference learning and coherent arbitrariness. J Environ Econ Manag 55:127–141. https://doi.org/10.1016/j.jeem.2007.08.003

Bierlaire M (2020) Biogeme. https://biogeme.epfl.ch/. Accessed 21 May 2020

Boeri M, Longo A (2017) The importance of regret minimization in the choice for renewable energy programmes: evidence from a discrete choice experiment. Energy Econ 63:253–260. https://doi.org/10.1016/j.eneco.2017.03.005

Boeri M, Scarpa R, Chorus CG (2014) Stated choices and benefit estimates in the context of traffic calming schemes: utility maximization, regret minimization, or both? Transp Res A Policy Pract 61:121–135. https://doi.org/10.1016/j.tra.2014.01.003

Braga J, Starmer C (2005) Preference anomalies, preference elicitation and the discovered preference hypothesis. Environ Resource Econ 32:55–89. https://doi.org/10.1007/s10640-005-6028-0

Brouwer R, Dekker T, Rolfe J, Windle J (2010) Choice certainty and consistency in repeated choice experiments. Environ Resource Econ 46:93–109. https://doi.org/10.1007/s10640-009-9337-x

Burrows J, Dixon P, Chan HM (2017) Response to cost prompts in stated preference valuation of environmental goods. In: McFadden D, Train K (eds) Contingent Valuation of Environmental Goods. Edward Elgar Publishing, pp 1–16

Cameron TA (1988) A new paradigm for valuing non-market goods using referendum data: maximum likelihood estimation by censored logistic regression. J Environ Econ Manag 15:355–379

Cameron TA, DeShazo JR (2010) Differential attention to attributes in utility-theoretic choice models. J Choice Model 3:73–115. https://doi.org/10.1016/S1755-5345(13)70015-0

Cameron TA, James MD (1987) Efficient estimation methods for "close-ended" contingent valuation surveys. the Review of Economics and Statistics 69:269–276

Campbell D, Boeri M, Doherty E, George Hutchinson W (2015) Learning, fatigue and preference formation in discrete choice experiments. J Econ Behav Organ 119:345–363. https://doi.org/10.1016/j.jebo.2015.08.018

Campbell D, Hensher DA, Scarpa R (2014) Bounding WTP distributions to reflect the "actual" consideration set. J Choice Model 11:4–15. https://doi.org/10.1016/j.jocm.2014.02.004

Campbell D, Hensher DA, Scarpa R (2011) Non-attendance to attributes in environmental choice analysis: a latent class specification. J Environ Planning Manage 54:1061–1076. https://doi.org/10.1080/09640568.2010.549367

Campbell D, Hutchinson WG, Scarpa R (2008) Incorporating discontinuous preferences into the analysis of discrete choice experiments. Environ Resource Econ 41:401–417. https://doi.org/10.1007/s10640-008-9198-8

Campbell D, Lorimer V (2009) Accommodating attribute processing strategies in stated choice analysis: do respondents do what they say they do? In: 17th European Association of Environmental and Resource Economists Annual Conference. Amsterdam

Campbell D, Mørkbak MR, Olsen SB (2018) The link between response time and preference, variance and processing heterogeneity in stated choice experiments. J Environ Econ Manage 88:18–34. https://doi.org/10.1016/j.jeem.2017.10.003

Caputo V, Loo EJV, Scarpa R et al (2018) Comparing serial, and choice task stated and inferred attribute non-attendance methods in food choice experiments. J Agric Econ 69:35–57. https://doi.org/10.1111/1477-9552.12246

Caputo V, Nayga RM, Scarpa R (2013) Food miles or carbon emissions? Exploring labelling preference for food transport footprint with a stated choice study. Aust J Agric Resource Econ 57:465–482. https://doi.org/10.1111/1467-8489.12014

Carlsson F, Frykblom P, Lagerkvist CJ (2007) Preferences with and without prices—does the price attribute affect behavior in stated preference surveys? Environ Resource Econ 38:155–164. https://doi.org/10.1007/s10640-006-9068-1

Carlsson F, Kataria M, Lampi E (2010) Dealing with ignored attributes in choice experiments on valuation of Sweden's environmental quality objectives. Environ Resource Econ 47:65–89. https://doi.org/10.1007/s10640-010-9365-6

Carlsson F, Martinsson P (2008a) How much is too much? Environ Resource Econ 40:165–176. https://doi.org/10.1007/s10640-007-9146-z

Carlsson F, Martinsson P (2008b) Does it matter when a power outage occurs?—A choice experiment study on the willingness to pay to avoid power outages. Energy Econ 30:1232–1245. https://doi.org/10.1016/j.eneco.2007.04.001

Carlsson F, Mørkbak MR, Olsen SB (2012) The first time is the hardest: a test of ordering effects in choice experiments. J Choice Model 5:19–37. https://doi.org/10.1016/S1755-5345(13)70051-4

Chalak A, Abiad M, Balcombe K (2016) Joint use of attribute importance rankings and non-attendance data in choice experiments. Eur Rev Agric Econ 43:737–760. https://doi.org/10.1093/erae/jbw004

Chater N, Oasksford M, Nakisa R, Redington M (2003) Fast, frugal, and rational: how rational norms explain behavior. Organ Behav Hum Decis Process 90:63–86. https://doi.org/10.1016/S0749-5978(02)00508-3

Chavez D, Palma M, Collart A (2018) Using eye-tracking to model attribute non-attendance in choice experiments. Appl Econ Lett 25:1355–1359. https://doi.org/10.1080/13504851.2017.1420879

Chorus C, van Cranenburgh S, Dekker T (2014) Random regret minimization for consumer choice modeling: assessment of empirical evidence. J Bus Res 67:2428–2436. https://doi.org/10.1016/j.jbusres.2014.02.010

References

Chorus CG (2012) Random regret-based discrete choice modeling: a tutorial. Springer-Verlag, Berlin Heidelberg

Chorus CG, Arentze TA, Timmermans HJP (2008) A random regret-minimization model of travel choice. Transp Res B Methodol 42:1–18. https://doi.org/10.1016/j.trb.2007.05.004

Chorus CG, Rose JM, Hensher DA (2013) Regret minimization or utility maximization: it depends on the attribute. Environ Plan B Plan Des 40:154–169. https://doi.org/10.1068/b38092

Collins AT, Hensher DA (2015) The influence of varying information load on inferred attribute non-attendance. In: Rasouli S, Timmermans HJP (eds) Bounded rational choice behaviour: applications in transport. Emerald Group Publishing, United Kingdom, pp 73–94

Czajkowski M (2020) Models for discrete choice experiments. https://github.com/czaj/dce. Accessed: 21 May 2020

Czajkowski M, Giergiczny M, Greene WH (2014) Learning and fatigue effects revisited: investigating the effects of accounting for unobservable preference and scale heterogeneity. Land Econ 90:324–351. https://doi.org/10.3368/le.90.2.324

Daniel AM, Persson L, Sandorf ED (2018) Accounting for elimination-by-aspects strategies and demand management in electricity contract choice. Energy Econ 73:80–90. https://doi.org/10.1016/j.eneco.2018.05.009

Dekker T, Chorus CG (2018) Consumer surplus for random regret minimisation models. J Environ Econ Policy 7:269–286. https://doi.org/10.1080/21606544.2018.1424039

DeShazo JR, Fermo G (2004) Implications of rationally-adaptive pre-choice behavior for the design and estimation of choice models. Working Paper 2004/8 University of California, Los Angeles 29

Deshazo JR, Fermo G (2002) Designing choice sets for stated preference methods: the effects of complexity on choice consistency. J Environ Econ Manag 44:123–143

Erdem S, Campbell D, Thompson C (2014) Elimination and selection by aspects in health choice experiments: prioritising health service innovations. J Health Econ 38:10–22. https://doi.org/10.1016/j.jhealeco.2014.06.012

Foster V, Mourato S (2002) Testing for consistency in contingent ranking experiments. J Environ Econ Manag 44:309–328. https://doi.org/10.1006/jeem.2001.1203

Gigerenzer G, Gaissmaier W (2011) Heuristic decision making. Annu Rev Psychol 62:451–482. https://doi.org/10.1146/annurev-psych-120709-145346

Glenk K, Martin-Ortega J, Pulido-Velazquez M, Potts J (2015) Inferring attribute non-attendance from discrete choice experiments: implications for benefit transfer. Environ Resource Econ 60:497–520. https://doi.org/10.1007/s10640-014-9777-9

Glenk K, Meyerhoff J, Akaichi F, Martin-Ortega J (2019) Revisiting cost vector effects in discrete choice experiments. Resource Energy Econ 57:135–155. https://doi.org/10.1016/j.reseneeco.2019.05.001

Hanley N, Adamowicz W, Wright RE (2005) Price vector effects in choice experiments: an empirical test. Resource Energy Econ 27:227–234. https://doi.org/10.1016/j.reseneeco.2004.11.001

Hanley N, Ryan M, Wright R (2003) Estimating the monetary value of health care: lessons from environmental economics. Health Econ 12:3–16. https://doi.org/10.1002/hec.763

Hensher DA (2006) Revealing differences in willingness to pay due to the dimensionality of stated choice designs: an initial assessment. Environ Resource Econ 34:7–44. https://doi.org/10.1007/s10640-005-3782-y

Hensher DA, Collins AT (2011) Interrogation of responses to stated choice experiments: is there sense in what respondents tell us?: A closer look at what respondents choose and process heuristics used in stated choice experiments. J Choice Model 4:62–89. https://doi.org/10.1016/S1755-5345(13)70019-8

Hensher DA, Collins AT, Greene WH (2013) Accounting for attribute non-attendance and common-metric aggregation in a probabilistic decision process mixed multinomial logit model: a warning on potential confounding. Transportation 40:1003–1020. https://doi.org/10.1007/s11116-012-9447-0

Hensher DA, Greene WH (2010) Non-attendance and dual processing of common-metric attributes in choice analysis: a latent class specification. Empirical Econ 39:413–426. https://doi.org/10.1007/s00181-009-0310-x

Hensher DA, Greene WH, Rose JM (2006) Deriving willingness-to-pay estimates of travel-time savings from individual-based parameters. Environ Plan A 38:2365–2376. https://doi.org/10.1068/a37395

Hensher DA, Puckett SM, Rose JM (2007a) Extending stated choice analysis to recognise agent-specific attribute endogeneity in bilateral group negotiation and choice: a think piece. Transportation 34:667–679. https://doi.org/10.1007/s11116-007-9124-x

Hensher DA, Rose J, Bertoia T (2007b) The implications on willingness to pay of a stochastic treatment of attribute processing in stated choice studies. Transp Res E Logist Transp Rev 43:73–89. https://doi.org/10.1016/j.tre.2005.07.006

Hensher DA, Rose J, Greene WH (2005) The implications on willingness to pay of respondents ignoring specific attributes. Transportation 32:203–222. https://doi.org/10.1007/s11116-004-7613-8

Hensher DA, Rose JM (2009) Simplifying choice through attribute preservation or non-attendance: Implications for willingness to pay. Transp Res E Logist Transp Rev 45:583–590. https://doi.org/10.1016/j.tre.2008.12.001

Hensher DA, Rose JM, Greene WH (2012) Inferring attribute non-attendance from stated choice data: implications for willingness to pay estimates and a warning for stated choice experiment design. Transportation 39:235–245. https://doi.org/10.1007/s11116-011-9347-8

Hess S, Beck MJ, Chorus CG (2014) Contrasts between utility maximisation and regret minimisation in the presence of opt out alternatives. Transp Res A Policy Pract 66:1–12. https://doi.org/10.1016/j.tra.2014.04.004

Hess S, Hensher DA (2010) Using conditioning on observed choices to retrieve individual-specific attribute processing strategies. Transp Res B Methodol 44:781–790. https://doi.org/10.1016/j.trb.2009.12.001

Hess S, Hensher DA (2013) Making use of respondent reported processing information to understand attribute importance: a latent variable scaling approach. Transportation 40:397–412. https://doi.org/10.1007/s11116-012-9420-y

Hess S, Palma D (2019) Apollo: A flexible, powerful and customisable freeware package for choice model estimation and application—ScienceDirect. J Choice Model 32:100170. https://doi.org/10.1016/j.jocm.2019.100170

Hess S, Rose JM (2012) Can scale and coefficient heterogeneity be separated in random coefficients models? Transportation 39:1225–1239. https://doi.org/10.1007/s11116-012-9394-9

Hess S, Shires J, Bonsall P (2013) A latent class approach to dealing with respondent uncertainty in a stated choice survey for fare simplification on bus journeys. Transp A Transp Sci 9:473–493. https://doi.org/10.1080/18128602.2011.609190

Hess S, Stathopoulos A, Daly A (2012) Allowing for heterogeneous decision rules in discrete choice models: an approach and four case studies. Transportation 39:565–591. https://doi.org/10.1007/s11116-011-9365-6

Hess S, Train K (2017) Correlation and scale in mixed logit models. J Choice Model 23:1–8. https://doi.org/10.1016/j.jocm.2017.03.001

Hole AR (2020) Stata modules. https://www.sheffield.ac.uk/economics/people/hole/stata/software.html. Accessed: 21 May 2020

Hole AR, Kolstad JR (2012) Mixed logit estimation of willingness to pay distributions: a comparison of models in preference and WTP space using data from a health-related choice experiment. Empir Econ 42:445–469. https://doi.org/10.1007/s00181-011-0500-1

Hole AR, Kolstad JR, Gyrd-Hansen D (2013) Inferred vs. stated attribute non-attendance in choice experiments: a study of doctors' prescription behaviour. J Econ Behav Organ 96:21–31. https://doi.org/10.1016/j.jebo.2013.09.009

Kahneman D, Tversky A (1979) Prospect theory: an analysis of decision under risk. Econometrica 47:263–291

References

Kaye-Blake WH, Abell WL, Zellman E (2009) Respondents' ignoring of attribute information in a choice modelling survey. Aust J Agric Resource Econ 53:547–564. https://doi.org/10.1111/j.1467-8489.2009.00467.x

Kim J, Rasouli S, Timmermans H (2017) Satisfaction and uncertainty in car-sharing decisions: an integration of hybrid choice and random regret-based models. Transp Res A Policy Pract 95:13–33. https://doi.org/10.1016/j.tra.2016.11.005

Kragt ME (2013) The effects of changing cost vectors on choices and scale heterogeneity. Environ Resource Econ 54:201–221. https://doi.org/10.1007/s10640-012-9587-x

Ladenburg J, Olsen SB (2008) Gender-specific starting point bias in choice experiments: evidence from an empirical study. J Environ Econ Manag 56:275–285. https://doi.org/10.1016/j.jeem.2008.01.004

Lagarde M (2013) Investigating attribute non-attendance and its consequences in choice experiments with latent class models. Health Econ 22:554–567. https://doi.org/10.1002/hec.2824

Leong W, Hensher DA (2012) Embedding multiple heuristics into choice models: an exploratory analysis. J Choice Model 5:131–144. https://doi.org/10.1016/j.jocm.2013.03.001

Mariel P, Meyerhoff J (2018) A more flexible model or simply more effort? On the use of correlated random parameters in applied choice studies. Ecol Econ 154:419–429. https://doi.org/10.1016/j.ecolecon.2018.08.020

McFadden D (1974) Conditional logit analysis of qualitative choice behaviour. In: Zarembka P (ed). Academic Press, New York, pp 105–142

Meyerhoff J, Glenk K (2015) Learning how to choose-effects of instructional choice sets in discrete choice experiments. Resource Energy Econ 41:122–142. https://doi.org/10.1016/j.reseneeco.2015.04.006

Mitchell RC, Carson RT (1989) Using surveys to value public goods: the contingent valuation method. RFF Press, Washington, D.C.

Mørkbak MR, Christensen T, Gyrd-Hansen D (2010) Choke price bias in choice experiments. Environ Resource Econ 45:537–551. https://doi.org/10.1007/s10640-009-9327-z

Mørkbak MR, Olsen SB, Campbell D (2014) Behavioral implications of providing real incentives in stated choice experiments. J Econ Psychol 45:102–116. https://doi.org/10.1016/j.joep.2014.07.004

Ohler T, Le A, Louviere J, Swait J (2000) Attribute range effects in binary response tasks. Market Lett 11:249–260. https://doi.org/10.1023/A:1008139226934

Rose JM, Hess S, Collins AT (2013) What if my model assumptions are wrong?: The impact of non-standard behaviour on choice model estimation. J Transp Econ Policy 47:245–263

Russo JE, Dosher BA (1983) Strategies for multiattribute binary choice. J Exp Psychol Learn Mem Cogn 9:676–696. https://doi.org/10.1037/0278-7393.9.4.676

Ryan M, Wordsworth S (2000) Sensitivity of willingness to pay estimates to the level of attributes in discrete choice experiments. Scottish J Polit Econ 47:504–524. https://doi.org/10.1111/1467-9485.00176

Sælensminde K (2006) Causes and consequences of lexicographic choices in stated choice studies. Ecol Econ 59:331–340. https://doi.org/10.1016/j.ecolecon.2005.11.001

Sandorf ED, Campbell D, Hanley N (2017) Disentangling the influence of knowledge on attribute non-attendance. J Choice Model 24:36–50. https://doi.org/10.1016/j.jocm.2016.09.003

Sarrias M, Daziano R (2017) Multinomial logit models with continuous and discrete individual heterogeneity in R: the gmnl package. J Stat Softw 79:1–46. https://doi.org/10.18637/jss.v079.i02

Scarpa R, Gilbride TJ, Campbell D, Hensher DA (2009a) Modelling attribute non-attendance in choice experiments for rural landscape valuation. Eur Rev Agric Econ 36:151–174. https://doi.org/10.1093/erae/jbp012

Scarpa R, Thiene M, Galletto L (2009b) Consumers wtp for wine with certified origin: preliminary results from latent classes based on attitudinal responses. J Food Prod Market 15:231–248. https://doi.org/10.1080/10454440902973377

Scarpa R, Thiene M, Hensher DA (2010) Monitoring choice task attribute attendance in nonmarket valuation of multiple park management services: does it matter? Land Econ 86:817–839

Scarpa R, Thiene M, Train K (2008) Utility in willingness to pay space: a tool to address confounding random scale effects in destination choice to the Alps. Am J Agr Econ 90:994–1010. https://doi.org/10.1111/j.1467-8276.2008.01155.x

Scarpa R, Zanoli R, Bruschi V, Naspetti S (2013) Inferred and stated attribute non-attendance in food choice experiments. Am J Agr Econ 95:165–180. https://doi.org/10.1093/ajae/aas073

Spinks J, Mortimer D (2016) Lost in the crowd? Using eye-tracking to investigate the effect of complexity on attribute non-attendance in discrete choice experiments. BMC Med Inform Decis Mak 16:14. https://doi.org/10.1186/s12911-016-0251-1

Swait J, Louviere J (1993) The role of the scale parameter in the estimation and comparison of multinomial logit models. J Mark Res 30:305–314. https://doi.org/10.1177/002224379303000303

Thaler RH (1999) Mental accounting matters. J Behav Decis Making 12:183–206. https://doi.org/10.1002/(SICI)1099-0771(199909)12:3%3c183::AID-BDM318%3e3.0.CO;2-F

Thiene M, Boeri M, Chorus CG (2012) Random regret minimization: exploration of a new choice model for environmental and resource economics. Environ Resource Econ 51:413–429. https://doi.org/10.1007/s10640-011-9505-7

Thiene M, Franceschinis C, Scarpa R (2019) Congestion management in protected areas: accounting for respondents' inattention and preference heterogeneity in stated choice data. Eur Rev Agric Econ 46:834–861. https://doi.org/10.1093/erae/jby041

Thiene M, Scarpa R (2009) Deriving and testing efficient estimates of WTP distributions in destination choice models. Environ Resource Econ 44:379–395. https://doi.org/10.1007/s10640-009-9291-7

Thiene M, Scarpa R, Louviere JJ (2015) Addressing preference heterogeneity, multiple scales and attribute attendance with a correlated finite mixing model of tap water choice. Environ Resource Econ 62:637–656. https://doi.org/10.1007/s10640-014-9838-0

Thiene M, Swait J, Scarpa R (2017) Choice set formation for outdoor destinations: the role of motivations and preference discrimination in site selection for the management of public expenditures on protected areas. J Environ Econ Manage 81:152–173. https://doi.org/10.1016/j.jeem.2016.08.002

Train K, Weeks M (2005) Discrete choice models in preference space and willingness-to-pay space. In: Scarpa R, Alberini A (eds) Springer. The Netherlands, Dordrecht, pp 1–16

Tversky A, Kahneman D (1974) Judgment under uncertainty: heuristics and biases. Science 185:1124–1131. https://doi.org/10.1126/science.185.4157.1124

Uggeldahl K, Jacobsen C, Lundhede TH, Olsen SB (2016) Choice certainty in discrete choice experiments: will eye tracking provide useful measures? J Choice Model 20:35–48. https://doi.org/10.1016/j.jocm.2016.09.002

Uggeldahl KC, Street C, Lundhede T, Olsen S (2017) Examining attribute non-attendance in discrete choice experiments using a gaze-contingent eye tracking application. International Choice Modelling Conference. Cape Town, South Africa

van Cranenburgh S (2020) Advanced random regret minimization models. https://www.advancedrrmmodels.com. Accessed: 21 May 2020

van Cranenburgh S, Chorus CG (2017) Does the decision rule matter for large-scale transport models? Transp Res Procedia 23:848–867. https://doi.org/10.1016/j.trpro.2017.05.047

van Cranenburgh S, Collins AT (2019) New software tools for creating stated choice experimental designs efficient for regret minimisation and utility maximisation decision rules. J Choice Model 31:104–123. https://doi.org/10.1016/j.jocm.2019.04.002

van Cranenburgh S, Rose JM, Chorus CG (2018) On the robustness of efficient experimental designs towards the underlying decision rule. Transp Res A Policy Pract 109:50–64. https://doi.org/10.1016/j.tra.2018.01.001

References

Waldman KB, Richardson RB (2018) Confronting tradeoffs between agricultural ecosystem services and adaptation to climate change in Mali. Ecol Econ 150:184–193. https://doi.org/10.1016/j.ecolecon.2018.04.003

Weller P, Oehlmann M, Mariel P, Meyerhoff J (2014) Stated and inferred attribute non-attendance in a design of designs approach. J Choice Model 11:43–56. https://doi.org/10.1016/j.jocm.2014.04.002

Open Access This chapter is licensed under the terms of the Creative Commons Attribution 4.0 International License (http://creativecommons.org/licenses/by/4.0/), which permits use, sharing, adaptation, distribution and reproduction in any medium or format, as long as you give appropriate credit to the original author(s) and the source, provide a link to the Creative Commons license and indicate if changes were made.

The images or other third party material in this chapter are included in the chapter's Creative Commons license, unless indicated otherwise in a credit line to the material. If material is not included in the chapter's Creative Commons license and your intended use is not permitted by statutory regulation or exceeds the permitted use, you will need to obtain permission directly from the copyright holder.

Chapter 7
Calculating Marginal and Non-marginal Welfare Measures

Abstract This chapter focuses on the calculation of marginal and non-marginal welfare measures. It outlines how the calculation of welfare measures is related to the specified model and the assumptions underlying that model. It further describes how the calculation of these measures is affected by the inclusion of preference heterogeneity, including the incorporation of interaction terms to capture observed preference heterogeneity or random parameters to capture unobserved preference heterogeneity. Finally, it discusses how these measures can be aggregated and compared.

7.1 Calculating Marginal Welfare Measures

WTP in the context of DCEs is defined as the amount of income a person is willing to give up for a certain improvement of an attribute or a combination of attributes, so that the overall change in utility is zero. Similarly, WTA is the minimum amount of extra income required to compensate for a certain deterioration of an attribute. WTP and WTA are based on microeconomic theory and correspond to the Hicksian welfare measures (see Sect. 1.1). Freeman et al. (2014, p. 68) describe these concepts in detail and Bateman et al. (2006) present the application of different welfare measures. This section will specifically focus on marginal WTP (mWTP), whereas Sect. 7.2 will discuss welfare implications of larger changes (e.g., in multiple attributes) and related issues of aggregation.

The concept of mWTP is defined as the marginal rate of substitution between the attribute and the price attribute in the indirect utility function and hence relates to the notion of indifference (Dekker 2014).

$$mWTP = -V'(a)/V'(c) \tag{7.1}$$

where a and c are the attribute of interest and the cost attribute, respectively and V' is the first partial derivative of the indirect utility function. For readability, indices for individuals, alternatives and choice situations are omitted. If the attributes enter utility linearly, the mWTP boils down to $mWTP = -\frac{\beta_a}{\beta_c}$, where β_a and β_c

are the corresponding parameters of the attribute of interest and the cost attribute, respectively.

When using models that incorporate interaction terms to capture observed preference heterogeneity, i.e. allowing marginal utilities of attributes to vary across people, some caution is required. Assume that we interact attribute a with a continuous, case-specific variable, e.g., age. As utility depends on age, so does mWTP. The value of mWTP is thus a function of age and can be conveniently written as

$$mWTP(age) = -V'(a)/V'(c) = -\frac{\beta_a + \beta_{a \cdot age} \cdot age}{\beta_c},$$

where $\beta_{a \cdot age}$ is the corresponding parameter of the interaction term. It is possible to substitute any possible value of age to calculate mWTP for that specific age. The ratio β_a/β_c will not provide a useful value as it would be the mWTP for a person of age zero. If the mean value of age can be taken as a representative value, it could be advisable to mean-centre this variable before the interaction is formed. Then the mean age would be zero, and the ratio β_a/β_c would represent the mWTP for the mean value of age. Nevertheless, in some cases other values of the case-specific variables (e.g. median value), can be more representative.

Further difficulties in calculating mWTP may arise when we specify the cost parameter as random in a RP-MXL model. This is because the ratio of two random variables follows a different, often unknown distribution. For some distributions, the first and second moments of the resulting ratio distribution are not defined, which makes it impossible to report means and standard deviations (Daly et al. 2012). For other distributions, moments may be defined but cannot be calculated analytically. If we are interested in knowing the shape of such a distribution, we can use simulation. The basic idea is to randomly draw from the distributions of the relevant random parameters and calculate mWTP for each draw (Krinsky and Robb 1986, 1991). See Daly et al. (2012, 2020) for the limitations of this approach.

If the random parameters are correlated, these correlations need to be taken into account when generating the random draws to compute their ratios. This is accommodated by drawing from a multivariate distribution. Such draws are feasible for two normally distributed random variables, yet it becomes more difficult if the any of the coefficients have a distributional form that is not a transformation of a normal distribution (Yang 2008). Hensher et al. (2015) recommend only drawing from the multivariate normal distribution.

Simulating the distributions has another advantage: it provides a good indication of whether the assumptions on the random parameters are meaningful. For example, a log-normally distributed cost coefficient may provide a good model fit. However, its large standard deviation may produce very unrealistic results. In a simulation, it can quickly become obvious that many mWTP values are not plausible (see Sect. 8.3 on cross-validation). A recent example of a study using this type of simulation is Knoefel et al. (2018). Simulation is, however, not the key solution because many problems with the resulting distribution can be masked.

7.1 Calculating Marginal Welfare Measures

The log-normal distribution is frequently used in RP-MXLs to specify the price coefficient. The distribution has the advantage that its values cannot become negative ($\exp(x) > 0, \forall x$). Similar to the normal distribution (and many other parametric distributions), the log-normal distribution is characterised by two parameters, the location parameter μ and the scale parameter σ. These parameters determine the shape of the distribution. In the normal distribution, μ and σ represent the mean (and the median as the distribution is symmetric) and the standard deviation of the distribution. In the log-normal distribution, the relevant statistics (median, mean and standard deviation) have to be calculated using the formulas presented in Sect. 5.4.

Note that the log-normal distribution is not symmetric, and the mean depends on σ. If σ is large (i.e. the distribution has a fat tail), the mean will quickly become (too) large as well. In such cases, it is useful to report the median as a central tendency measure. In our experience, the median provides, in many cases, a more useful value (Daly et al. 2012). Recent examples for median WTP values from log-normal distributions are Sagebiel et al. (2017) and Rommel and Sagebiel (2017). Note that most statistical software packages output μ and σ, and the researcher has to calculate mean, median and standard deviation using the above-mentioned formulas. For policy and welfare analysis however, it is helpful to report the distribution of mWTP, especially, when the distribution does not follow a clearly defined shape.

Finally, RP-MXL models allow the calculation of so-called individual-specific (conditional) utility parameters and mWTP values (Train 2009, Chap. 11; Sarrias 2020). This approach is useful when the researcher aims to predict future choices for specific individuals or when individuals are used for subsequent analysis. However, these conditional values are only meaningful with a sufficiently large number of choices per individual, depending on the complexity of the choice tasks. Also, blocked designs may cause imprecise conditional estimates as individuals faced different sequences of choices. As a consequence, following this approach may only be recommended when it is necessary for a follow-up analysis.

The value of mWTP in a LCM can be calculated for each class separately, using the standard approach $mWTP_l = -V'_l(a)/V'_l(c)$ where l denotes the class $l = (1, \ldots, L)$. The value usually reported is the weighted mean of the within-class mWTP values weighted by the class share.

$$mWTP_w = \sum_{l=1}^{L} classShare_l \cdot mWTP_l$$

The literature that uses this formula is vast as it is applied in almost all case studies based on LCM, but let us mention for example Scarpa and Thiene (2005).

mWTP is a key concept in welfare economics and rooted in microeconomic theory. Some microeconomic background is required to fully understand the concept of mWTP. While simple model specifications allow a straightforward and easy calculation and interpretation of mWTP, researchers need to be careful once specifications become more complicated. Most importantly, non-centred interaction terms can easily lead to a misinterpretation. Similarly, when using RP-MXL models with randomly distributed cost coefficients, calculation and interpretation become more complicated.

Nearly all empirical applications in environmental economics rely on mWTP, even in contexts where welfare effects are not the main subject. In the latter cases, mWTP serves as a way of obtaining a meaningful interpretation of results and some kind of importance ranking. As mWTP in RP-MXL models is rather difficult to obtain, many studies investigated this topic. A good summary is provided in Hensher et al. (2015). A detailed, and somewhat advanced discussion of mWTP for random cost parameters is Daly et al. (2012). Conditional mWTP values are described in detail in Train (2009, Chap. 11). In general, practitioners should look into distributions of mWTP rather than specific statistics (mean, median, standard deviation), and only use those models where a meaningful interpretation of mWTP is feasible. Researchers should double check if the mWTP distributions are realistic. If a large percentage of the distribution falls outside the range of acceptable values (e.g. mWTP for renewable energy per kWh is more than 1€, or a yearly payment for water quality improvements of 10,000 €), something may be wrong, even if model fit statistics indicate differently.

7.2 Aggregating Welfare Effects

Often researchers are not interested in the welfare implications of marginal changes, but wish to derive the monetary value of a policy intervention (or product change). Policy interventions often involve changes in multiple attributes and of a reasonable but non-marginal size. Economic theory provides the tools to derive such values. First, we need to establish the do-nothing scenario and the corresponding utility level for each individual, denoted by V_0. Any policy intervention, assuming a quality improvement, will increase the utility to V_1. Effectively, we are interested in the value of the utility difference $V_1 - V_0$ for each individual and the aggregation of these individual effects. This is exactly what the Hicksian welfare measures do (see Sect. 1.1).

A key issue with discrete choice modelling is, however, that a priori we do not know which goods individuals will select in the do-nothing scenario and whether they would switch as a result of the policy change. We typically work with what is known as the LogSum (Ben-Akiva and Lerman 1985), which denotes the expected maximum utility of a choice set here denoted for the do-nothing scenario—where j denotes an alternative in the choice set:

$$LS_0 = \ln\left(\sum_j \exp(V_{j0})\right).$$

The change in the expected maximum utility as a result of the policy intervention is then denoted by:

7.2 Aggregating Welfare Effects

$$LS_1 - LS_0 = \ln\left(\sum_j \exp(V_{j1})\right) - \ln\left(\sum_j \exp(V_{j0})\right).$$

Utility is, however, not informative for cost–benefit purposes and we require a translation into monetary terms using the marginal utility of income λ. Batley and Ibáñez Rivas (2013) highlight that when the indirect utility function is linear in income and price, we can use the negative of the cost coefficient β_c for this purpose, i.e. $\lambda = -\beta_c$, such that the monetary change in e.g. compensating surplus is denoted by:

$$\Delta CS = \frac{LS_1 - LS_0}{\lambda}.$$

When the discrete choice model is linear in both the non-cost *and* cost attributes, the LogSum, i.e. the change in compensating surplus, is identical to the sum of the constant marginal WTP estimates for the individual attributes. When non-linear non-cost attributes are introduced, aggregation over non-marginal quality improvements is far less trivial than simply deriving the change in the LogSum for a given scenario. Hence, the use of the LogSum is recommended in such instances.

The introduction of non-linear costs in the indirect utility functions causes significant theoretical and computational challenges. The issue here is that due to the inclusion of non-linear cost effects the marginal utility of income is no longer constant and thus invalidates the use of the LogSum in these cases. Batley and Dekker (2019) show that in a discrete choice setting non-linear cost effects are non-compatible with economic theory, despite the fact that an econometric model may suggest that non-linear costs are likely. Karlstrom and Morey (2003) and McFadden (1996) have developed methods to derive the resulting change in "compensating variation" using methods of integration and simulation, respectively. These methods are hardly implemented in the literature due to their challenging computational burden.

The LogSum thus allows the change in compensating surplus to be derived for a given individual. However, we are typically interested what the policy intervention implies for the population and not the sample. When mWTP estimates are used, such as the case for the Value of Statistical Life (Robinson and Hammitt 2016) one can simply use these as a multiplier as stated in national cost–benefit analysis guidelines such as the Green Book in the UK (HM Treasury 2018). Alternatively, one can derive the welfare implications for different representative socio-economic groups using the estimated indirect utility functions and the LogSum and aggregate over the population. Essentially, this will indicate whether the net WTP is positive or negative for society, and thus be a reflection of the Kaldor and Hicks compensation criteria. However, Nyborg (2014) highlights there are significant controversial value judgements made when simply aggregating WTP and WTA across people. She argues that effectively more weight is given to richer people in the social welfare analysis as a result.

To sum up, firstly, the output of discrete choice models is commonly a set of mWTP measures. These are not always informative when quality effects are non-linear in the indirect utility function. Secondly, the LogSum facilitates aggregation of welfare effects, particularly versus the do-nothing scenario. Thirdly, more complicated calculations are required when non-linearities are associated with income and price variables.

7.3 WTP Comparison

In some applications, it is interesting to compare welfare measures from different samples. For example, a researcher has collected two samples from different cities and wants to find out if WTP is larger in one city than in another city. Or the researcher has conducted a split sample to answer a specific methodical question and wants to find out whether there is a difference in the two samples. Direct testing with t-tests is not appropriate, as welfare measures such as mWTP are ratios of coefficients (non-linear combinations) and they are, therefore, usually non-normally distributed. One way to test differences by comparing simulated distributions. The idea is to simulate mWTP values and count in how many cases the mWTP value from one sample is larger than that from the other sample. This procedure has been proposed by Poe et al. (1994, 2005). A step-by-step guide can be found in Haab and McConnell (2002, p. 112).

The Poe test can be conducted for basically any model including RP-MXL models, but be aware that mean and median mWTP are sometimes calculated from the location and scale parameters (e.g. for log-normally distributed price coefficients, see Sect. 7.1), which requires a different formula for mWTP. One can use Poe test to compare other welfare measures such as compensating surplus of a specific policy scenario. The process is similar to that with mWTP, with the only difference that, for each draw, the compensating surplus formula is used instead of the mWTP formula.

If the Poe test is not feasible, or a formal test is not required, one can conduct a graphical analysis of confidence intervals. Plotting mean mWTP and their respective confidence intervals of two samples offer a good initial insight into the magnitude of the differences. When confidence intervals overlap, mWTP are not likely to be statistically different. Note that both in the Poe test and in the overlapping confidence interval approach, the null hypothesis of equality of mWTP is less likely to be rejected the larger the variations and confidence intervals are.

In summary, comparing independent samples with respect to welfare measures can be done with the Poe et al. (2005) test or with the overlapping confidence interval method. Several empirical applications rely on the Poe test to establish if there are differences in WTP between samples. See, for example, Liebe et al. (2015) or Glenk et al. (2019) for methodological applications, and Brouwer et al. (2010, 2016) and Knoefel et al. (2018) for empirical applications.

References

Bateman IJ, Day BH, Georgiou S, Lake I (2006) The aggregation of environmental benefit values: welfare measures, distance decay and total WTP. Ecol Econ 60:450–460. https://doi.org/10.1016/j.ecolecon.2006.04.003

Batley R, Dekker T (2019) The intuition behind income effects of price changes in discrete choice models, and a simple method for measuring the compensating variation. Environ Resource Econ. https://doi.org/10.1007/s10640-019-00321-2

Batley R, Ibáñez Rivas JN (2013) Applied welfare economics with discrete choice models: implications of theory for empirical specification. In: Hess S, Daly A (eds) Choice modelling. Edward Elgar Publishing, pp 144–171

Ben-Akiva M, Lerman S (1985) Discrete choice analysis. theory and applications to travel demand. The MIT Press, Cambridge, MA

Brouwer R, Bliem M, Getzner M et al (2016) Valuation and transferability of the non-market benefits of river restoration in the Danube river basin using a choice experiment. Ecol Eng 87:20–29. https://doi.org/10.1016/j.ecoleng.2015.11.018

Brouwer R, Martin-Ortega J, Berbel J (2010) Spatial preference heterogeneity: a choice experiment. Land Econ 86:552–568. https://doi.org/10.3368/le.86.3.552

Daly A, Hess S, Train K (2012) Assuring finite moments for willingness to pay in random coefficient models. Transportation 39:19–31. https://doi.org/10.1007/s11116-011-9331-3

Daly A, Hess S, Ortúzar J (2020) Estimating willingness-to-pay from discrete choice models: setting the record straight. Working paper. Choice Modelling Centre (CMC). University of Leeds. https://www.stephanehess.me.uk/publications.html

Dekker T (2014) Indifference based value of time measures for Random Regret Minimisation models. J Choice Model 12:10–20. https://doi.org/10.1016/j.jocm.2014.09.001

Freeman AMI, Herriges JA, Kling CL (2014) The measurement of environmental and resource values : theory and methods. Routledge

Glenk K, Meyerhoff J, Akaichi F, Martin-Ortega J (2019) Revisiting cost vector effects in discrete choice experiments. Resource Energy Econ 57:135–155. https://doi.org/10.1016/j.reseneeco.2019.05.001

Haab TC, McConnell KE (2002) Valuing environmental and natural resources. The econometrics of non-market valuation. Edward Elgar Publishing Limited, Cheltenham, UK

Hensher DA, Rose JM, Greene WH (2015) Applied choice analysis, 2nd edn. Cambridge University Press, Cambridge

HM Treasury (2018) The green book: central government guidance on appraisal and evaluation. OGL Press, London, UK

Karlstrom A, Morey ER (2003) Calculating the exact compensating variation in logit and nested-logit models with income effects: theory, intuition, implementation, and application. Social Science Research Network, Rochester, NY

Knoefel J, Sagebiel J, Yildiz Ö et al (2018) A consumer perspective on corporate governance in the energy transition: evidence from a Discrete Choice Experiment in Germany. Energy Econ 75:440–448. https://doi.org/10.1016/j.eneco.2018.08.025

Krinsky I, Robb A (1986) On approximating the statistical properties of elasticities. Rev Econ Stat 68:715–719. https://doi.org/10.2307/1924536

Krinsky I, Robb AL (1991) Three methods for calculating the statistical properties of elasticities: a comparison. Empirical Econ 16:199–209. https://doi.org/10.1007/BF01193491

Liebe U, Glenk K, Oehlmann M, Meyerhoff J (2015) Does the use of mobile devices (tablets and smartphones) affect survey quality and choice behaviour in web surveys? J Choice Model 14:17–31. https://doi.org/10.1016/j.jocm.2015.02.002

McFadden D (1996) Computing willingness-to-pay in random utility models. University of California at Berkeley, Econometrics Laboratory Software Archive

Nyborg K (2014) Project evaluation with democratic decision-making: what does cost–benefit analysis really measure? Ecol Econ 106:124–131. https://doi.org/10.1016/j.ecolecon.2014.07.009

Poe GL, Giraud KL, Loomis JB (2005) Computational methods for measuring the difference of empirical distributions. Am J Agr Econ 87:353–365. https://doi.org/10.1111/j.1467-8276.2005.00727.x

Poe GL, Severance-Lossin EK, Welsh MP (1994) Measuring the difference (X-Y) of simulated distributions: a convolutions approach. Am J Agr Econ 76:904–915. https://doi.org/10.2307/1243750

Robinson LA, Hammitt JK (2016) Valuing reductions in fatal illness risks: implications of recent research. Health Econ 25:1039–1052. https://doi.org/10.1002/hec.3214

Rommel K, Sagebiel J (2017) Preferences for micro-cogeneration in Germany: policy implications for grid expansion from a discrete choice experiment. Appl Energy 206:612–622. https://doi.org/10.1016/j.apenergy.2017.08.216

Sagebiel J, Glenk K, Meyerhoff J (2017) Spatially explicit demand for afforestation. Forest Policy Econ 78:190–199. https://doi.org/10.1016/j.forpol.2017.01.021

Sarrias M (2020) Individual-specific posterior distributions from Mixed Logit models: properties, limitations and diagnostic checks. Journal of Choice Modelling 100224. https://doi.org/10.1016/j.jocm.2020.100224

Scarpa R, Thiene M (2005) Destination choice models for rock climbing in the Northeastern Alps: a latent-class approach based on intensity of preferences. Land Econ 81:426–444

Train K (2009) Discrete choice methods with simulation, 2nd edn. Cambridge University Press, New York

Yang M (2008) Normal log-normal mixture, leptokurtosis and skewness. Appl Econ Lett 15:737–742. https://doi.org/10.1080/13504850600749073

Open Access This chapter is licensed under the terms of the Creative Commons Attribution 4.0 International License (http://creativecommons.org/licenses/by/4.0/), which permits use, sharing, adaptation, distribution and reproduction in any medium or format, as long as you give appropriate credit to the original author(s) and the source, provide a link to the Creative Commons license and indicate if changes were made.

The images or other third party material in this chapter are included in the chapter's Creative Commons license, unless indicated otherwise in a credit line to the material. If material is not included in the chapter's Creative Commons license and your intended use is not permitted by statutory regulation or exceeds the permitted use, you will need to obtain permission directly from the copyright holder.

Chapter 8
Validity and Reliability

Abstract This chapter concerns different aspects of validity and reliability of a discrete choice experiment. Firstly, it focuses on three essential concepts for assessing the validity of the welfare estimates obtained in the choice experiment, namely content, construct and criterion validity. Secondly, it discusses how the reliability of the recorded choices can be assessed. It then discusses issues related to model comparison and selection. Finally, it addresses prediction in discrete choice models as a way to assess the quality of a model.

8.1 The Three Cs: Content, Construct and Criterion Validity

While goodness-of-fit measures and prediction success may be used to assess the validity of the econometric model, broader aspects of validity of the obtained value estimates should also be assessed when conducting DCE surveys. In general, the overarching goal of most applied environmental DCE surveys is to provide welfare measures that mirror as accurately as possible the actual values of the target population. A DCE survey with the highest level of validity would be one that produces WTP estimates that are identical to the true WTPs in the population. However, given that true values cannot be observed for non-marketed environmental changes, such a direct and simple test of the validity of a DCE survey is not available. Instead, the validity of welfare measures obtained from a DCE survey will have to be assessed through more indirect indicators. Different classifications of validity testing can be found in the valuation literature as well as in the broader survey literature (e.g. Bateman et al. 2002; Scherpenzeel and Saris 1997). In a recent paper, Bishop and Boyle (2019) present an overview and a useful framework for considering validity as well as reliability of non-market valuation surveys. They outline three different aspects of validity, referred to as "the Three Cs": content validity, construct validity and criterion validity. All three are important for assessing the validity of welfare estimates obtained from an environmental DCE survey.

Content validity concerns the extent to which the chosen valuation method, as well as all aspects of its practical implementation, is appropriate and conducive for obtaining a measure of the true value. This involves assessing to what extent all the various components of the DCE survey (e.g. questionnaire development, the questions asked, scenario descriptions, survey information, attributes included, survey mode, sampling of respondents, etc.) have induced respondents to make choices that are in line with their true preferences. Content validity assessment may also consider the extent to which the analysis of choices and reporting of results are conducted in a way that appropriately conveys valid welfare estimates to relevant end users, e.g. decision- and policymakers. The assessment of content validity is inherently based on a great deal of subjective judgements and for a large part it basically relies on the analyst's common sense and accumulated experience and expertise.

Construct validity focuses more on the construct of interest, namely the value estimates and how the validity of these might be assessed in the absence of knowledge about the true values. One key element of construct validity is the so-called expectation-based validity. Often the analyst will have some prior expectations of the values and how they relate to other variables. One source of such expectations is economic theory. According to economic theory, the marginal utility of income is positive, though decreasing with increasing income. This presents two theoretical expectations that can and should be tested in DCE surveys. Most importantly, the parameter estimate for the cost (price) attribute should be significantly negative since paying money is equal to giving up income which according to the underlying economic theory implies a loss of utility. In other words, keeping everything else constant, increasing the cost of an alternative should decrease the probability of choosing that alternative. Estimating an insignificant or even a positive cost parameter would seriously invalidate the results of a DCE survey. Hence, this is probably the most crucial validity test that any DCE survey has to pass. An associated validity test concerns the decreasing marginal utility of income. Again keeping everything else constant, this implies that a respondent with relatively low income should be more sensitive to the cost of an alternative than a respondent with relatively high income. If there is sufficient income variation in the respondent sample, this can be tested, for example, by incorporating interactions between the cost attribute and dummy variables for income brackets. The parameter estimate for such an interaction should be significant, and the sign would depend on which income bracket is described by the incorporated dummy. For other non-cost attributes, there might also be expectations based on economic theory. Of particular relevance is what may be considered an internal test of sensitivity to scope. The non-satiation axiom of consumer preferences basically means that more consumption is always better than less consumption. Hence, if for instance people have positive preferences for the conservation of endangered species, and we use an attribute in a DCE to describe three different levels of species conservation (e.g. 10, 100 and 1000 species protected), one would expect $WTP(10) < WTP(100) < WTP(1000)$, or at least $WTP(10) \leq WTP(100) \leq WTP(1000)$.

Another source of expectations for construct validity tests could be intuition or past research experiences. For instance, given the plethora of water quality valuation studies concluding that people have positive WTP for improvements in water quality, one would expect to find a significantly positive parameter estimate for an attribute describing improvements in water quality. These types of validity tests should probably be considered less strict than those based on economic theory. There could be good reasons why a specific study might not find the same findings as other studies, e.g. if the target population differs. This would obviously not be as serious as finding out that the underlying economic theory assumptions were violated, but some good explanations would be warranted.

A somewhat different test of construct validity is the so-called convergent validity (see, e.g., Hoyos and Riera 2013). When previously conducted valuation studies, using DCE or other valuation methods, have been designed to estimate the same value as the DCE currently being conducted, the value estimates should be statistically similar. Thus, when discussing the results of a new DCE survey, it is common practice to compare WTP estimates to previous estimates of WTP for the same or similar type of good, if available. If results are statistically indistinguishable, such a convergence of results may be interpreted as an indication of construct validity. This relates to the expectation-based validity mentioned above relying on past research experiences. If one is conducting a new DCE investigating preferences for water quality improvements, the obtained WTP estimates should be compared to (some of) the many previous WTP estimates available in the literature. It is important to note, though, that even if WTP estimates are similar in two or more surveys, this does not guarantee that valid estimates of the true WTPs have been obtained. For instance, a DCE and a CVM survey might produce similar WTP estimates for a water quality improvement, but they may both suffer from hypothetical bias. Furthermore, if WTP estimates are found to differ significantly from previous estimates, can we conclude that either the new or the previous WTP estimates are biased? Or are they both biased, but to differing degrees? This underlines the importance of considering all the three Cs.

The last of the three Cs refers to criterion validity. This idea is quite similar to that of convergent validity, namely comparing the WTP estimates obtained in a new DCE survey to previously obtained WTP estimates for the same good. The main difference is that the previous WTP estimates have been obtained with a method that is generally considered to provide highly valid estimates of true WTP. Ideally, this benchmark would be market prices but this is obviously not relevant for non-marketed goods. A second-best solution is to look towards simulated markets or laboratory or field experiments involving actual economic transactions, see, e.g., Carlsson and Martinsson (2001) and Murphy et al. (2005), which is commonly considered to be of higher validity than purely hypothetical settings. In practice, however, such experiments involving actual payments for non-marketed environmental goods are quite rare, simply because they are often not possible to construct. Hence, quite often when considering WTP for environmental goods, criterion validity is impossible to assess.

To sum up, it is generally recommended to thoroughly consider the three Cs of validity at all stages of environmental DCE surveys—from initial conceptualisation and survey design through to data collection and analysis. The purpose here is to ensure as far as possible that the estimated values will reflect the population's actual values for the described environmental change. The three Cs are equally important in the final stage; reporting results to end users. The aim here is to prove to end users that the generated value estimates are valid. For most environmental valuation contexts, it is not known what the true values are—and this is the motivation for conducting a DCE in the first place. Hence, end users' validity assessments will inherently be quite subjective, based on whatever information is available to them. It is therefore recommended to report as much detail as possible about the background for the value estimates, thus essentially enabling end users to make their own assessments of the content validity. Carefully describe questionnaire development, data collection, and analysis, and make sure results are discussed thoroughly in relation to previous findings as well as theory-based or case-specific expectations. If reporting results in scientific journals or other outlets with page- or word-limits, it is recommended to provide supplementary material online. This includes the full questionnaire used for data collection as well as summary reports from focus groups and pilot testing. The sampling strategy, a detailed analysis of representativeness and econometric analysis may also be reported here in more detail than in the main report or paper. Though not yet standard practice, in the spirit of reproducibility it is also recommended to make data as well as code used to generate reported WTP estimates available to others in permanent and freely accessible repositories.

8.2 Testing Reliability

Reliability and validity determine the accuracy of estimates of welfare change derived using valuation methods. Both reliability and validity are often described with the metaphor of shooting arrows at a target, as in archery. Reliability implies that arrows are grouped closely together. This does not mean the arrows have hit the bullseye or are even close to it. To the contrary, reliability may be found if arrows are consistently off target, but in the same direction. Low reliability therefore means that repeated shots at the target are dispersed widely across the target. Validity, then, measures how close the arrows are to the bullseye. Therefore, in the words of Bishop and Boyle (2019, p. 560), "reliability is about variance and validity is about bias". Relating the metaphor above to choice experiments, a shot at the target is like conducting a survey to generate an estimate of welfare change (say, of average WTP for an environmental improvement). It should be emphasised that this section is concerned about the reliability of a method, choice experiments, to obtain such a welfare estimate, and not about the reliability of the welfare measure (e.g. compensating variation) per se.

Typical valuation studies only permit a single "shot" at the target, i.e. a single survey. In this case, nothing can be said about the reliability of choice experiments as a method to derive estimates of welfare change. The main procedure used in social science to assess the reliability of survey-based measurements is to conduct a test-retest study (Yu 2005; Liebe et al. 2012). Ideally, the same subjects conduct the same task, e.g. responding to a survey or participating in an experiment, at two (or more)

8.2 Testing Reliability

points in time, and provide independent observations. Therefore, instead of having only one shot at the target, now there are two (or more). Statistical tests can then be used to test the hypothesis of equality with respect to measures or indicators that the tested methods are supposed to provide.

In the context of choice experiments, a test-retest experiment implies conducting the same survey again, at different points in time, i.e. conducting several survey waves at points in time $t, t + 1, \ldots, t + n$ where n defines the time lag between survey waves. This can be done with the same subjects (within-subject test-retest), who ideally then answer exactly the same choice sets; or, if within-subject tests are not possible, the retest is undertaken with a different sample from the same population (between-subject test-retest). Within-subject tests are considered advantageous over between-subject tests, although there are challenges regarding the assumption that observations at two (or more) points in time are indeed independent. We will discuss this further below. Moreover, there is an implicit (i.e. not typically tested or controlled for) assumption that respondents answer the surveys at different points in time under the same circumstances. However, this may or may not be the case. Given that most test-retest studies are conducted using a web survey mode, let us consider a web survey. A respondent may complete it in a busy workplace environment on a desktop PC in the first wave and on a mobile phone while relaxing on the sofa at home at the weekend in the second wave.

As of now, test-retest studies in the choice experiment literature consider some or all of the measures of test-retest reliability listed below. It should be noted that these also apply to comparisons of choice consistency within the same survey wave (e.g. Brouwer et al. 2017; Czajkowski et al. 2016), which is, however, not the focus of this section.

(a) Tests of congruence (or consistency) of choices for data collected in different survey waves. Such tests can comprise congruence of choice of alternatives, across the whole sample, blocks of the experimental design or for individual choice sets, and the number of congruent choices that each individual respondent made.
(b) Tests of equality of parameter vectors and, if equality of parameter vectors cannot be rejected, equality of error variance between survey waves.
(c) Tests of equality of mean WTP (or WTP distributions) between survey waves.

Different statistical tests are used to assess the above dimensions of test–retest reliability. For example, Brouwer et al. (2017) use a Sign test for equality of choices, Liebe et al. (2012) a test of symmetry of test and retest choices proposed by Bowker (1948). Mørkbak and Olsen (2015) and Matthews et al. (2017) test general agreement of choices taking into account that respondents may choose the same alternative in two waves by chance using a correction factor for random matching, Cohen's κ (Cohen 1968). Mørkbak and Olsen (2015), Rigby et al. (2016) and Brouwer et al. (2017) use a parametric approach to explain choice consistency using panel data probit models.

Equality of parameter vectors across survey waves is typically tested following the Swait and Louviere (1993) procedure. Comparisons of mean WTP estimates across surveys conducted at different points in time can be based on a Krinsky and Robb (1986, 1991) procedure followed by the complete combinatorial test proposed by Poe et al. (2005), or Wald tests in case estimates are derived from models in WTP space rather than preference space models (Czajkowski et al. 2016; Brouwer et al. 2017). In addition to testing for equality of mean WTP distributions, Czajkowski et al. (2016) test for equality of variances in derived WTP distributions.

Findings across the half dozen or so applications of test-retest reliability in choice experiments in the environmental economics literature provide a mixed picture that, however, tends to rather suggest that choice experiments can provide reliable welfare estimates. Additional test-retest choice experiment studies can be found in the health economics literature, for example Bryan et al. (2000) and San Miguel et al. (2002). The following summary focuses on differences in WTP estimates across survey waves only. In a between-subject test-retest study with a time lag between survey waves of one year, Bliem et al. (2012) report no significant differences in WTP. Liebe et al. (2012) provide a within-subject test-retest study with survey waves being eleven months apart and find significant differences in WTP only for one attribute level. Czajkowski et al. (2016) find that means of WTP distributions are relatively stable over time (lag of six months), while variances are found to differ. They argue, however, that accounting for preference heterogeneity and correlations of random parameters is a more stringent test of preference equality across time periods. Comparing results of surveys conducted with a time lag of one year between survey waves, Schaafsma et al. (2014) report that mean WTP estimates were not found to be significantly different at the 5% level, but that estimates of compensating variation for policy scenarios can differ significantly. Rigby et al. (2016) and Mørkbak and Olsen (2015) find a relatively high degree of inter-temporal preference stability and choice consistency for $t + 1 = 6$ months and $t + 1 = 2$ weeks, respectively. Matthews et al. (2017) and Brouwer et al. (2017) each compare results for three survey waves, each wave being three months apart (Matthews et al. 2017) and six as well as 24 months after the initial survey wave (Brouwer et al. 2017). Both Matthews et al. (2017) and Brouwer et al. (2017) report significant differences in WTP estimates across survey waves. Brouwer et al. (2017) also provide a comparison of test-test reliability for choice experiment and open-ended SP question formats.

What may drive potential differences in choice consistency and preferences across time? An intuitive suspicion is that there were changes in the composition and/or characteristics of the sample, which had an influence on preferences; for example, income or education may have changed over time, or a participant has become more or less environmentally concerned. Therefore, all test-retest studies need to carefully control for potential differences in sample characteristics and/or composition over time. This highlights some of the trade-offs in choosing the time interval between survey waves. If the interval is very short, we can be reasonably confident that characteristics such as income or general environmental concern will not have changed between time periods. The longer the interval, the greater the likelihood that such factors have changed, and the greater the chance that unobserved and thus uncontrolled factors affecting preferences affect the test-retest "experiment". However, shorter intervals between survey waves make it more likely that respondents remember their answers to the previous survey, or are influenced by their previous experience with the same survey. This would then question the independence of observations obtained from the same respondents across survey waves. Generally, test-retest studies may be subject to effects resulting from preference learning as analysed in Plott (1993) and in the context of unfamiliar public goods in Brouwer (2012). This most likely context dependent learning effect may or may not be invariant to the time lag between survey waves.

Another aspect related to the independence of observations across survey waves is experience in responding to choice experiment surveys and associated institutional learning. That is, respondents may learn how to evaluate choice alternatives and associated attribute trade-offs. However, institutional learning should theoretically only impact on error variance and not affect preference parameters. Respondents' engagement with a survey may also be affected if they realise that they are being asked to respond to the exact same survey again. Again, one could argue that this may affect primarily choice consistency and hence error variance rather than preferences. However, it is conceivable that repeating the survey again may affect perceived consequentiality, which in turn may affect WTP. This will depend on how the repeat survey is introduced to respondents.

A number of studies have investigated factors influencing the likelihood of choice consistency in terms of congruence of choices facing the same choice tasks across survey waves (e.g. Mørkbak and Olsen 2015; Rigby et al. 2016; Brouwer et al. 2017). Aspects that were found to matter include choice complexity (e.g. using the entropy measure of complexity suggested by Swait and Adamowicz 2001), response times, cognitive capability of respondents, respondents' experience with a good and measures of respondents' stated certainty regarding choices.

It is important to note that it is more likely that the null hypothesis of differences between survey rounds in test-retest experiments is rejected if the variance of variables and parameter estimates that serve as measures of reliability increases. This is a function of sample size and other factors. Therefore, all else being equal, studies with larger samples are implicitly less likely to confirm test-retest reliability using the statistical tests mentioned above, while their internal estimates (i.e. estimates for each survey round) are actually more reliable. Concerning other factors that affect variance, this may for example include whether the information provided in the valuation scenario is clear and can be understood in a similar way by all survey respondents. In this way, a survey that contains confusing information on valuation scenarios (e.g. attribute and attribute level descriptions) is actually more likely to statistically confirm test-retest reliability than a survey where this information is provided in a clear and concise manner that has been thoroughly pretested for understanding using qualitative methods such as focus groups and "think aloud" protocols.

Given the multitude of potentially relevant factors influencing choices and thus choice consistency over time, clearly it is actually quite challenging to infer general statements on the reliability of the choice experiment method to obtain welfare estimates from a single test-retest experiment (Bishop and Boyle 2019). This may ultimately change as more test-retest studies of choice experiments become available.

8.3 Comparing Models

An important step when modelling discrete choices is the selection process of models which should be presented in e.g. a journal paper. Authors usually only present a few models, although they may have estimated 20 or 30 different models with different specifications. There are several ways to compare models, yet it is difficult to come up with a straightforward and unambiguous model choice (see, e.g., Sagebiel 2017 for a review of methods when choosing between an RP-MXL and an LCM). The data generating process is unknown and all efforts to identify the "true" model are—to some extent—speculative. In many cases, researchers base their decisions on statistical measures-of-fit and test results, and argue that the presented models are those that seem to fit the data best. However, model choice can also be based on the research question and the specific goals of the study. For example, if the sample size is low and the research interest is on preference heterogeneity, it may be pragmatic to go for a parsimonious RP-MXL or LCM rather than a highly parameterised LCRP-MXL model with error components (Train 2009). If the focus is on prediction, it may be a good idea to estimate a model with many parameters of which some have no theoretical or behavioural underpinning. Note, however, that in most applications in environmental economics, the focus is not on prediction. If the focus is on testing a theoretically derived hypothesis, a parsimonious model can be a better choice, as it is less prone to overfitting and multicollinearity. To break this down, choosing a model is ultimately based on the researcher's own judgement, which is informed by several, sometimes contrasting criteria and the purpose of the research. As George Box puts it, "all models are wrong, but some are useful" (Box 1979, p. 202). Hence, the researcher's task is to select the most useful model for a given dataset, purpose and context.

There are two main strategies to compare models statistically. The first strategy is based on the estimated log-likelihood values and gives information on how well a model explains the observed data (i.e. the data used to estimate the model). However, it does not tell us how well the model explains/predicts choices. Basing model choice only on model fit bears the risk of *overfitting* a model. An overfitted model explains the observed data very well—but only the observed data. An overfitted model applied to a new data set likely performs worse than a more parsimonious model. The broad term *cross validation* describes a set of methods to identify how the estimated model performs in predicting out-of-sample choices.

Whichever route a researcher chooses, a first step should always be a visual inspection of the models. Are the parameters plausible? Do the models provide reasonable welfare estimates and meaningful distributions of WTP? By just looking at the model output, it may be possible to quickly detect inconsistencies in certain models.

8.3.1 Model Fit-Based Strategies to Choose Among Different Models

The easiest and quickest way to compare models is by looking at the log-likelihood value, the Pseudo R^2 and information criteria such as the Bayesian Information Criteria (BIC) and the Akaike Information Criteria (AIC). Finally, statistical tests can be used to find out whether a larger log-likelihood value in one model is statistically significantly larger than in the other model.

Goodness-of-fit measures are used for a general description of how well the model fits the data. The most widely used measure of the goodness-of-fit of discrete choice models is McFadden's pseudo-R^2, defined as

$$McFadden\ pseudo\text{-}R^2 = 1 - \frac{\ln L}{\ln L_0},$$

where $\ln L$ is the likelihood function value at convergence and $\ln L_0$ is the likelihood function value of the model including only alternative specific constants for all alternatives but one. Since it is always in the range [0, 1] and higher values represent a better fit, it is somewhat similar to the R^2 statistic from linear models but note that the values of McFadden's pseudo-R^2 do not have a direct interpretation. Therefore, the value of McFadden's pseudo-R^2 is largely meaningless and it is unknown if, for example, 0.2 represents a "good" or "poor" model fit (Greene 2017). In recent years, more appealing alternatives have been proposed, such as Tjur's pseudo-R^2 (Tjur 2009).

A related approach for assessing the fit of the model and for comparing competing models is based on measures of information. In this regard, the information theory-founded AIC is commonly used:

$$AIC = -2 \ln L + 2K,$$

where K is the number of parameters in the model. An alternative measure is the Bayesian (Schwarz) Information Criterion

$$BIC = -2 \ln L + K \ln N,$$

which imposes a higher penalty for a larger number of parameters (N). Note that these measures are not limited to be in the 0–1 range and lower values represent a better model fit. It is typical to report normalised AIC and BIC values, that is, divided by the number of observations. It is worth noting that although the goodness-of-fit measures can be compared between models to describe which model fits better, it is not possible to judge if the improvement in model fit is statistically significant or not.

There are several tests that can be used to compare model fit. The likelihood ratio test can be used to compare nested models. It is possible to test a conditional logit model against an RP-MXL, but it is not possible to test RP-MXL models against LCMs (as these are non-nested). A rarely used test to compare non-nested models has been proposed by Ben-Akiva and Swait (1986). This test is based on the AIC and provides a χ^2 statistic that (an arbitrary) Model 2 is the true model. An application of the test is provided, for example, in Sagebiel (2017).

8.3.2 Cross Validation

Cross validation, in general, refers to validating the model by applying the model to data which had not been used in model estimation. One simple strategy is to delete one observation from the sample, estimate the model and see how the model predicts for the *left-out* observation. This exercise is repeated several times and the average prediction error is calculated. The key advantage of this "leave-one-out" test is that it provides a very accurate estimate of how good the model performs in terms of robustness, as the whole data is used for estimation. The disadvantage of the leave-one-out test is that it is computationally intensive, as the same model has to be re-estimated several times. Therefore, it is appropriate for smaller samples and simple models. An alternative strategy is to randomly drop a certain percentage of the observations, and estimate the model without the dropped observations (hold-out sample). The estimated parameters are then used to predict the choices of the excluded observations. The number of correct predictions can be used as an indication of how well the model performs outside of the sample. This procedure is less computationally intensive than the leave-one-out test, because each model is estimated only once. The hold-out sample approach is therefore more adequate for larger samples and computationally intensive models. Although cross validation is less frequently used in environmental DCE applications, it is a very powerful way to investigate the ability of a model to predict and to identify overfitted models (Bierlaire 2016).

Choosing the correct model is a difficult task and requires researchers to inspect the model results from different perspectives. While the purpose of the research can guide model choice, statistical criteria should always be taken into account and reported. Likelihood-based measures and tests as well as cross validation are useful tools. However, no selection criteria identifies "the correct" model. In the end, it is down to the researcher's own judgement to select a model.

8.4 Prediction

Generally, a researcher does not have enough information to accurately predict an individual's choice. Therefore, choice models can only predict the probability that the individual will choose an alternative but not the individual's choice. The percentage of individuals in the sample for which the highest-probability alternative and the chosen alternative coincide is called the per cent correctly predicted or simply hit rate.

It is important to bear in mind that predicting choice probabilities means that if the choice situation were repeated numerous times, each alternative would be chosen a certain proportion of the time. However, this does not mean that the alternative with the highest probability will be chosen each time. An individual can choose an alternative with the lowest probability in a specific choice occasion because of factors not observed by the researcher. This is why a widely used goodness-of-fit measure based on the "percent correctly predicted" should be avoided as it is opposed to the concept of probability. It assumes that the choice is perfectly predicted by the researcher by choosing the alternative for which the model gives the highest probability.

In some fields, the common approach towards forecasting is to estimate the best possible model and use it to predict the choices that lead to a prediction of quantity of interest based on the individual choices. This is a typical goal, for example, in transportation or marketing. Nevertheless, seeking an excellent in-sample fit can lead to an overfitted model that cannot offer much confidence in terms of out-of-sample forecast ability. In environmental valuation, the main focus is usually on the WTP values or welfare measures based on the estimated coefficients and not on predicted choices. Notwithstanding, if the alternatives are assigned to a specific environmental programme or action, the individual predictions can be relevant to identify appropriate policies.

Regarding the prediction of the probabilities of choosing an alternative, the literature mentions various problems related to this. The list includes, for example, the uncertainty in future alternatives, aggregation, or the aforementioned, overfitting. The aggregation problem can appear across individuals, alternatives or time. Discrete choice models are usually estimated at the level of individual decision-makers (allowing for heterogeneity and interdependencies among individuals) but the predicted quantity is aggregated (e.g. market share, average response to a policy change). The consistent way of aggregating over individuals is sample enumeration (Train 2009). To find a trade-off between the best model fit and models with the highest predictive performance is a relatively difficult task. A comprehensive description of the problems related to prediction in the choice models can be found in Habibi (2016).

References

Bateman IJ, Carson RT, Day BH et al (2002) Economic valuation with stated preferences techniques: a manual. Edward Elgar, Cheltenham

Ben-Akiva M, Swait J (1986) The akaike likelihood ratio index. Transp Sci 20:133–136. https://doi.org/10.1287/trsc.20.2.133

Bierlaire M (2016) Common mistakes in discrete choice modeling. Episode 2: Survival of the fittest... or not. https://www.youtube.com/watch?v=_w7RxZIUBqI&t=127s. Accessed 12 May 2020

Bishop RC, Boyle KJ (2019) Reliability and validity in nonmarket valuation. Environ Resource Econ 72:559–582. https://doi.org/10.1007/s10640-017-0215-7

Bliem M, Getzner M, Rodiga-Laßnig P (2012) Temporal stability of individual preferences for river restoration in Austria using a choice experiment. J Environ Manage 103:65–73. https://doi.org/10.1016/j.jenvman.2012.02.029

Bowker AH (1948) A test for symmetry in contingency Tables. J Am Stat Assoc 43:572–574. https://doi.org/10.1080/01621459.1948.10483284

Box GEP (1979) Robustness in the strategy of scientific model building. In: Launer RL, Wilkinson GN (eds) Robustness in statistics. Academic Press, pp 201–236

Brouwer R (2012) Constructed preference stability: a test–retest. J Environ Econ Policy 1:70–84. https://doi.org/10.1080/21606544.2011.644922

Brouwer R, Logar I, Sheremet O (2017) Choice consistency and preference stability in test-retests of discrete choice experiment and open-ended willingness to pay elicitation formats. Environ Resource Econ 68:729–751. https://doi.org/10.1007/s10640-016-0045-z

Bryan S, Gold L, Sheldon R, Buxton M (2000) Preference measurement using conjoint methods: an empirical investigation of reliability. Health Econ 9:385–395. https://doi.org/10.1002/1099-1050(200007)9:5%3c385::AID-HEC533%3e3.0.CO;2-W

Carlsson F, Martinsson P (2001) Do Hypothetical and actual marginal willingness to pay differ in choice experiments?: Application to the valuation of the environment. J Environ Econ Manag 41:179–192. https://doi.org/10.1006/jeem.2000.1138

Cohen J (1968) Weighted kappa: nominal scale agreement with provision for scaled disagreement or partial credit. Psychol Bull 70:213–220

Czajkowski M, Barczak A, Budziński W et al (2016) Preference and WTP stability for public forest management. Forest Policy Econ 71:11–22. https://doi.org/10.1016/j.forpol.2016.06.027

Greene WH (2017) Econometric analysis, 8th edn. Pearson, New York, NY

Habibi S (2016) Prediction-driven approaches to discrete choice models with application to forecasting car type demand. Doctoral Thesis in Transport Science, KTH Royal Institute of Technology

Hoyos D, Riera P (2013) Convergent validity between revealed and stated recreation demand data: some empirical evidence from the Basque Country, Spain. J Forest Econ 19:234–248. https://doi.org/10.1016/j.jfe.2013.02.003

Krinsky I, Robb A (1986) On approximating the statistical properties of elasticities. Rev Econ Stat 68:715–719. https://doi.org/10.2307/1924536

Krinsky I, Robb AL (1991) Three methods for calculating the statistical properties of elasticities: a comparison. Empirical Econ 16:199–209. https://doi.org/10.1007/BF01193491

Liebe U, Meyerhoff J, Hartje V (2012) Test-retest reliability of choice experiments in environmental valuation. Environ Resource Econ 53:389–407. https://doi.org/10.1007/s10640-012-9567-1

Matthews Y, Scarpa R, Marsh D (2017) Stability of willingness-to-pay for coastal management: a choice experiment across three time periods. Ecol Econ 138:64–73. https://doi.org/10.1016/j.ecolecon.2017.03.031

Mørkbak MR, Olsen SB (2015) A within-sample investigation of test–retest reliability in choice experiment surveys with real economic incentives. Aust J Agric Resour Econ 59:375–392. https://doi.org/10.1111/1467-8489.12067

Murphy JJ, Allen PG, Stevens TH, Weatherhead D (2005) A meta-analysis of hypothetical bias in stated preference valuation. Environ Resource Econ 30:313–325

Plott CR (1993) Rational individual behavior in markets and social choice processes. Social Science Working Paper, 862. California Institute of Technology, Pasadena, CA

Poe GL, Giraud KL, Loomis JB (2005) Computational methods for measuring the difference of empirical distributions. Am J Agr Econ 87:353–365. https://doi.org/10.1111/j.1467-8276.2005.00727.x

References

Rigby D, Burton M, Pluske J (2016) Preference stability and choice consistency in discrete choice experiments. Environ Resource Econ 65:441–461. https://doi.org/10.1007/s10640-015-9913-1

Sagebiel J (2017) Preference heterogeneity in energy discrete choice experiments: a review on methods for model selection. Renew Sustain Energy Rev 69:804–811. https://doi.org/10.1016/j.rser.2016.11.138

San Miguel F, Ryan M, Scott A (2002) Are preferences stable? The case of health care. J Econ Behav Organ 48:1–14. https://doi.org/10.1016/S0167-2681(01)00220-7

Schaafsma M, Brouwer R, Liekens I, De Nocker L (2014) Temporal stability of preferences and willingness to pay for natural areas in choice experiments: a test–retest. Resour Energy Econ 38:243–260. https://doi.org/10.1016/j.reseneeco.2014.09.001

Scherpenzeel AC, Saris WE (1997) the validity and reliability of survey questions: a meta-analysis of MTMM Studies. Sociol Methods Res 25:341–383. https://doi.org/10.1177/0049124197025003004

Swait J, Adamowicz W (2001) Choice environment, market complexity, and consumer behavior: a theoretical and empirical approach for incorporating decision complexity into models of consumer choice. Organ Behav Hum Decis Process 86:141–167. https://doi.org/10.1006/obhd.2000.2941

Swait J, Louviere J (1993) The role of the scale parameter in the estimation and comparison of multinomial logit models. J Mark Res 30:305–314. https://doi.org/10.1177/002224379303000303

Tjur T (2009) Coefficients of determination in logistic regression models—a new proposal: the coefficient of discrimination. Am Stat 63:366–372. https://doi.org/10.1198/tast.2009.08210

Train K (2009) Discrete choice methods with simulation, 2nd edn. Cambridge University Press, New York

Yu CH (2005) Test-retest reliability. In: Kempf-Leonard K (ed) Encyclopedia of social measurement. Elsevier, New York, pp 777–784

Open Access This chapter is licensed under the terms of the Creative Commons Attribution 4.0 International License (http://creativecommons.org/licenses/by/4.0/), which permits use, sharing, adaptation, distribution and reproduction in any medium or format, as long as you give appropriate credit to the original author(s) and the source, provide a link to the Creative Commons license and indicate if changes were made.

The images or other third party material in this chapter are included in the chapter's Creative Commons license, unless indicated otherwise in a credit line to the material. If material is not included in the chapter's Creative Commons license and your intended use is not permitted by statutory regulation or exceeds the permitted use, you will need to obtain permission directly from the copyright holder.

Chapter 9
Software

Abstract This chapter describes and compares suitable software for the analysis of basic and advanced discrete choice models. Software packages are classified into proprietary and non-proprietary, according to the operating system required and modelling capabilities. Abilities of both selected commercial (Stata, SAS and Latent Gold, e.g.) and open-source packages (Biogeme and R-libraries) are considered. Finally, some user-written estimation packages for Gauss, Matlab, R and Stata are presented.

There are many software packages for statistical computing and data analysis but not so many for the analysis of basic and advanced discrete choice models. The general statistical software packages can be classified into proprietary and non-proprietary (open-source, public-domain, freeware), by the operating system support (Windows, Mac OS, Linux, BSD, Unix, Cloud) or whether they are menu driven or non-menu driven.

The computing capabilities of new technologies and the dramatic increase of users and disciplines in which discrete choice has been used over the last two decades have positively influenced the number of software packages available today. Writing own codes of complex discrete choice models could and still can only be done by experienced users. Given that open-source and freeware concepts are relatively new, historically the commercial packages were very successful in spite of their limitations regarding the possibility for customisation or delays in the incorporation of the latest methodological approaches. The pioneers worth mentioning in this regard are Limdep-Nlogit (2016) and Alogit (2016). Other commercial packages that include more advanced discrete choice models are Stata (2019), SAS (2020) or Latent Gold (2020). All these commercial packages differ with respect to pricing, estimation speed, possibilities of various model options (constraints, covariates), flexibility of data structures (varying number of choice tasks or alternatives per individual), modelling in preference or WTP-space or the availability of other models.

Probably the most prominent examples for open-source packages are Biogeme (Bierlaire 2020) and several libraries in R (R Core Team 2020). Biogeme is an open-source Python package designed for the maximum likelihood estimation of parametric models in general, with a special emphasis on discrete choice models

(Bierlaire 2020). There are several versions of Biogeme that have been developed over the years (Gnu, Bison, Python, Pandas). The latest version called Pandas Biogeme is not a standalone executable, but a Python package. The package is written in Python, with the exception of the core calculations of the models written in C++ for the sake of efficiency. The management of the data relies on the Python data analysis library Pandas, which has become the workhorse of data scientists in recent years.

There are several R packages (libraries) available for the estimation for the discrete choice models. The mlogit (Croissant 2013) package belongs to the oldest and it includes only some extensions of MNL such as nested logit or heteroskedastic logit. The mnlogit (Hasan et al. 2016) package provides significant speed improvements over mlogit with very fast computations of the Hessian of the log-likelihood function. Therefore, it is preferable for the estimation of large-scale multiclass classification problems. Another, more flexible package for large-scale models is the mixl (Molloy 2020) package. It reduces markedly both the memory usage and runtime of the estimation allowing for estimation of more complex models such as MXL and HCM. The gmnl (Sarrias and Daziano 2017) package is one of the most complete packages offering estimation of a wide scale of models including MNL, MXL, G-MXL, and the mixed-mixed multinomial logit. It also offers many different post-estimation analysis procedures. Apollo (Hess and Palma 2019) is currently one of the most flexible packages as it allows estimation of a wide range of models and is fully customisable to support many more. Finally, the RSGHB (Dumont et al. 2019) package allows for estimation of MNL, RP- MXL, EC-MXL, LCM and Nested Logit by the use of the Hierarchical Bayesian framework.

In addition, there are many user-written estimation packages for Matlab, R, Gauss, Ox, C and others. These are typically available from researchers' websites or public repositories. MATLAB codes for estimation of a wide variety of discrete choice models can be found at Czajkowski (2020) or Train (2020). Similarily Gauss codes are at Train (2020b). Some STATA codes for numerous choice models and different postestimation analysis are at Hole (2020). Codes for RRM estimation can be found at very comprehensive website created by van Cranenburgh (2020). It includes codes for Pandas Biogeme, Apollo R, Python Biogeme, Bison Biogeme, MATLAB and Latent Gold.

The advantages of user-written estimation packages include the possibility of studying and modifying the code (e.g. to come up with a new specification). Some of them are also much faster and more precise than commercial packages. Finally, even though the simulated maximum likelihood is the preferred estimator of most researchers dealing with discrete choice models, some of the user-written packages offer the possibility of using other estimation frameworks, such as Bayesian framework (Train and Sonnier 2005), Expectation–Maximisation (EM) algorithm (Train 2007), Laplace approximation (Harding and Hausman 2007) or Maximum Approximate Composite Marginal Likelihood (Bhat and Sidharthan 2011). However, the EM algorithm is also used, in combination with Newton–Raphson, in Latent Gold, for example.

Many commercial packages are menu-driven and that make it easy for the user to input data, estimate a model and get some results. They are therefore usually a first step for beginners and will often be sufficient for many practical purposes. One drawback of this is that they are typically less concerned with the quality of the estimation. This could be problematic, particularly with more complex models (e.g. HCM, models in WTP-space, RP-MXL with correlated parameters). Experienced users tend to switch to user-written packages in R or MATLAB. In addition to greater estimation speed (partially through parallel computing) and higher flexibility of the model specification, they offer the possibility to choose from a wide selection of optimisers, investigate convergence criteria, use different strategies for starting values, etc. to make sure that the results are robust. The applied optimiser is an important issue when estimating nonlinear models, determining speed, robustness and precision.

When focusing on just speed and precision, Czajkowski et al. (2018) compare some of the available estimation packages. They found that in their specific setting their MATLAB implementation outperforms other packages, with R being approximately 5–10 times slower, Python Biogeme—approximately 20 times slower, NLOGIT—60 times slower and Stata—over 100 times slower.

Beginners should start with software that offers a user-friendly interface and gain some experience in the estimation of discrete choice models before moving on to more advance settings. The aforementioned packages offer a wide scale of models and practitioners who stick to standard models can pick the most convenient one. Advanced practitioners looking for the newest methodological approaches will probably code their own estimation procedures. For both groups, it is advisable to not only rely on one package but to estimate models in two environments and compare results. This is, of course, less important when MNL models are estimated but becomes more important when more complex models are estimated and the optimisers and starting values used in the estimation process become more influential.

Researchers should always bear in mind that the code for estimating models is a key part of his or her research. McCullough and Vinod (2003, p. 888) state that "Replication is the cornerstone of science. Research that cannot be replicated is not science, and cannot be trusted either as part of the profession's accumulated body of knowledge or as a basis for policy". Apart from replicability, that is repeating an entire study, independently of the original investigator without the use of original data, the reproducibility should be always guaranteed. A reproducibility seems to be an easy requirement to fulfil because it requires that we can take the original data and the computer code and reproduce all of the numerical outcomes from the study. Nevertheless, it is not, because the researchers are not always careful when organising and documenting their research.

So far not many journals publishing papers concerned with environmental valuation require that the data and estimation code are made available to readers. In other sciences, replicability is regarded as a fundamental principle for research and it should also be a top priority for the environmental valuation research agenda. Even if the journals in which we publish do not require the publication of code and data we should use other methods to make them public. This should be done in spite of the difficulties such as the time it takes to make the research reproducible, knowing that code and data are not universally recognised as research products or that there is not a well-established etiquette for working with code written by other researchers. Finally, the markdown concept of using dynamic analysis documents brings together modelling, documentation and publishing which helps to improve the replicability of research findings. Markdown software is available for R (rmarkdown) or Stata (markstat), for example.

References

Alogit (2016) ALOGIT 4.3. ALOGIT Software & Analysis Ltd. www.alogit.com

Bhat CR, Sidharthan R (2011) A simulation evaluation of the maximum approximate composite marginal likelihood (MACML) estimator for mixed multinomial probit models. Transp Res B Methodol 45:940–953. https://doi.org/10.1016/j.trb.2011.04.006

Bierlaire M (2020) Biogeme. https://biogeme.epfl.ch/. Accessed 21 May 2020

Croissant Y (2013) mlogit: Multinomial Logit models. Version 1.0-3.1URL https://CRAN.R-project.org/package=mlogit

Czajkowski M (2020) Models for discrete choice experiments. https://github.com/czaj/dce. Accessed: 21 May 2020

Czajkowski M, Buczyński M, Budziński W (2018) Replicability, simulation error and robustness to non-parametric treatment of preference heterogeneity in discrete choice models. In: The 25'th Ulvön Conference on Environmental Economics. 20.06.2018. Ulvön

Dumont J, Keller J, Carpenter C (2019) RSGHB: functions for hierarchical bayesian estimation: a flexible approach. Version 1.2.2URL https://CRAN.R-project.org/package=RSGHB

Harding MC, Hausman J (2007) Using a Laplace approximation to estimate the random coefficients logit model by nonlinear least squares. Int Econ Rev 48:1311–1328. https://doi.org/10.1111/j.1468-2354.2007.00463.x

Hasan A, Wang Z, Mahani AS (2016) Fast estimation of multinomial logit models: R package mnlogit. J Stat Softw 75:1–24. https://doi.org/10.18637/jss.v075.i03

Hess S, Palma D (2019) Apollo: a flexible, powerful and customisable freeware package for choice model estimation and application—ScienceDirect. J Choice Model 32:100170. https://doi.org/10.1016/j.jocm.2019.100170

Hole AR (2020) Stata modules. https://www.sheffield.ac.uk/economics/people/hole/stata/software.html. Accessed: 21 May 2020

Latent Gold (2020) Statistical Innovations, Arlington, USA. https://www.statisticalinnovations.com/. Accessed 12 June 2020

LIMDEP (2016) LIMDEP, Econometric Software, Inc. https://www.limdep.com/. Accessed 12 June 2020

McCullough BD, Vinod HD (2003) Verifying the solution from a nonlinear solver: a case study. Am Econ Rev 93:873–892. https://doi.org/10.1257/000282803322157133

Molloy J (2020) mixl: simulated maximum likelihood estimation of mixed logit models for large datasets. Version 1.1.2URL https://CRAN.R-project.org/package=mixl

R Core Team (2020) R: a language and environment for statistical computing. R Foundation for Statistical Computing, Vienna, Austria. https://www.R-project.org/

Sarrias M, Daziano R (2017) Multinomial logit models with continuous and discrete individual heterogeneity in R: the gmnl package. J Stat Softw 79:1–46. https://doi.org/10.18637/jss.v079.i02

SAS (2020) SAS Institute Inc., Cary, NC, USA. https://www.sas.com/. Accessed 12 June 2020

StataCorp (2019) Stata statistical software: Release 16. StataCorp LLC, College Station, TX

Train K (2020a) MATLAB codes. https://eml.berkeley.edu/~train/software.html. Accessed: 21 May 2020

References

Train K (2020b) GAUSS codes. https://eml.berkeley.edu/~train/software.html. Accessed: 21 May 2020

Train K (2007) A recursive estimator for random coefficient models

Train K, Sonnier G (2005) Mixed logit with bounded distributions of correlated partworths. In: Scarpa R, Alberini A (eds) Springer. The Netherlands, Dordrecht, pp 1–16

van Cranenburgh S (2020) Advanced random regret minimization models. https://www.advancedrrmmodels.com. Accessed: 21 May 2020

Open Access This chapter is licensed under the terms of the Creative Commons Attribution 4.0 International License (http://creativecommons.org/licenses/by/4.0/), which permits use, sharing, adaptation, distribution and reproduction in any medium or format, as long as you give appropriate credit to the original author(s) and the source, provide a link to the Creative Commons license and indicate if changes were made.

The images or other third party material in this chapter are included in the chapter's Creative Commons license, unless indicated otherwise in a credit line to the material. If material is not included in the chapter's Creative Commons license and your intended use is not permitted by statutory regulation or exceeds the permitted use, you will need to obtain permission directly from the copyright holder.